About the Author

Deke McClelland is the author of more than 30 books about desktop publishing and graphics programs for the Mac and Windows, including IDG's best-selling *Macworld Photoshop 3 Bible, Photoshop 3 For Macs For Dummies, CorelDRAW! 5 For Dummies, Macworld FreeHand 4 Bible,* and *PageMaker 5 For Windows For Dummies.*

He is also a contributing editor to *Macworld* magazine and frequently pops up in *Publish* and *PC World*. His awards include the Ben Franklin Award for the Best Computer Book of 1989 as well as two Computer Press Awards, one in 1990 and the other in 1992. When he isn't writing, he hosts the television series "Digital Gurus" for the Jones Computer Network. In his few minutes of spare time, he lives with his wife and aging cat in Boulder, Colorado.

Welcome to the world of IDG Books Worldwide.

IDG Books Worldwide, Inc., is a subsidiary of International Data Group, the world's largest publisher of computer-related information and the leading global provider of information services on information technology. IDG was founded more than 25 years ago and now employs more than 7,200 people worldwide. IDG publishes more than 233 computer publications in 65 countries (see listing below). More than sixty million people read one or more IDG publications each month.

Launched in 1990, IDG Books Worldwide is today the #1 publisher of best-selling computer books in the United States. We are proud to have received 3 awards from the Computer Press Association in recognition of editorial excellence, and our best-selling *...For Dummies™* series has more than 12 million copies in print with translations in 25 languages. IDG Books, through a recent joint venture with IDG's Hi-Tech Beijing, became the first U.S. publisher to publish a computer book in the People's Republic of China. In record time, IDG Books has become the first choice for millions of readers around the world who want to learn how to better manage their businesses.

Our mission is simple: Every IDG book is designed to bring extra value and skill-building instructions to the reader. Our books are written by experts who understand and care about our readers. The knowledge base of our editorial staff comes from years of experience in publishing, education, and journalism — experience which we use to produce books for the '90s. In short, we care about books, so we attract the best people. We devote special attention to details such as audience, interior design, use of icons, and illustrations. And because we use an efficient process of authoring, editing, and desktop publishing our books electronically, we can spend more time ensuring superior content and spend less time on the technicalities of making books.

You can count on our commitment to deliver high-quality books at competitive prices on topics consumers want to read about. At IDG, we value quality, and we have been delivering quality for more than 25 years. You'll find no better book on a subject than an IDG book.

John Kilcullen
President and CEO
IDG Books Worldwide, Inc.

IDG Books Worldwide, Inc., is a subsidiary of International Data Group, the world's largest publisher of computer-related information and the leading global provider of information services on information technology. International Data Group publishes over 220 computer publications in 65 countries. More than fifty million people read one or more International Data Group publications each month. The officers are Patrick J. McGovern, Founder and Board Chairman; Kelly Conlin, President; Jim Casella, Chief Operating Officer. International Data Group's publications include: **ARGENTINA'S** Computerworld Argentina, Infoworld Argentina; **AUSTRALIA'S** Computerworld Australia, Computer Living, Australian PC World, Australian Macworld, Network World, Mobile Business Australia, Publish!, Reseller, IDG Sources; **AUSTRIA'S** Computerwelt Oesterreich, PC Test; **BELGIUM'S** Data News (CW); **BOLIVIA'S** Computerworld; **BRAZIL'S** Computerworld, Connections, Game Power, Mundo Unix, PC World, Publish, Super Game; **BULGARIA'S** Computerworld Bulgaria, PC & Mac World Bulgaria, Network World Bulgaria; **CANADA'S** CIO Canada, Computerworld Canada, InfoCanada, Network World Canada, Reseller; **CHILE'S** Computerworld Chile, Informatica; **COLOMBIA'S** Computerworld Colombia, PC World; **COSTA RICA'S** PC World; **CZECH REPUBLIC'S** Computerworld, Elektronika, PC World; **DENMARK'S** Communications World, Computerworld Danmark, Computerworld Focus, Macintosh Produktkatalog, Macworld Danmark, PC World Danmark, PC Produktguide, Tech World, Windows World; **ECUADOR'S** PC World Ecuador; **EGYPT'S** Computerworld (CW) Middle East, PC World Middle East; **FINLAND'S** MikroPC, Tietoviikko, Tietoverkko; **FRANCE'S** Distributique, GOLDEN MAC, InfoPC, Le Guide du Monde Informatique, Le Monde Informatique, Telecoms & Reseaux; **GERMANY'S** Computerwoche, Computerwoche Focus, Computerwoche Extra, Electronic Entertainment, Gamepro, Information Management, Macwelt, Netzwelt, PC Welt, Publish, Publish; **GREECE'S** Publish & Macworld; **HONG KONG'S** Computerworld Hong Kong, PC World Hong Kong; **HUNGARY'S** Computerworld SZT, PC World; **INDIA'S** Computers & Communications; **INDONESIA'S** Info Komputer; **IRELAND'S** ComputerScope; **ISRAEL'S** Beyond Windows, Computerworld Israel, Multimedia, PC World Israel; **ITALY'S** Computerworld Italia, Lotus Magazine, Macworld Italia, Networking Italia, PC Shopping Italy, PC World Italia; **JAPAN'S** Computerworld Today, Information Systems World, Macworld Japan, Nikkei Personal Computing, SunWorld Japan, Windows World; **KENYA'S** East African Computer News; **KOREA'S** Computerworld Korea, Macworld Korea, PC World Korea; **LATIN AMERICA'S** GamePro; **MALAYSIA'S** Computerworld Malaysia, PC World Malaysia; **MEXICO'S** Compu Edicion, Compu Manufactura, Computacion/Punto de Venta, Computerworld Mexico, MacWorld, Mundo Unix, PC World, Windows; **THE NETHERLANDS'** Computer! Totaal, Computable (CW), LAN Magazine, Lotus Magazine, MacWorld; **NEW ZEALAND'S** Computer Buyer, Computerworld New Zealand, Network World, New Zealand PC World; **NIGERIA'S** PC World Africa; **NORWAY'S** Computerworld Norge, Lotusworld Norge, Macworld Norge, Maxi Data, Networld, PC World Ekspress, PC World Nettverk, PC World Norge, PC World's Produktguide, Publish& Multimedia World, Student Data, Unix World, Windowsworld; **PAKISTAN'S** PC World Pakistan; **PANAMA'S** PC World Panama; **PERU'S** Computerworld Peru, PC World; **PEOPLE'S REPUBLIC OF CHINA'S** China Computerworld, China Infoworld, China PC Info Magazine, Computer Fan, PC World China, Electronics International, Electronics Today/Multimedia World, Electronic Product World, China Network World, Software World Magazine, Telecom Product World; **PHILIPPINES'** Computerworld Philippines, PC Digest (PCW); **POLAND'S** Computerworld Poland, Computerworld Special Report, Networld, PC World/Komputer, Sunworld; **PORTUGAL'S** Cerebro/PC World, Correio Informatico/Computerworld, MacIn; **ROMANIA'S** Computerworld, PC World, Telecom Romania; **RUSSIA'S** Computerworld-Moscow, Mir - PK (PCW), Sety (Networks); **SINGAPORE'S** Computerworld Southeast Asia, PC World Singapore; **SLOVENIA'S** Monitor Magazine; **SOUTH AFRICA'S** Computer Mail (CIO),Computing S.A.,Network World S.A., Software World; **SPAIN'S** Advanced Systems, Amiga World, Computerworld Espana, Communicaciones World, Macworld Espana, NeXTWORLD, Super Juegos Magazine (GamePro), PC World Espana, Publish; **SWEDEN'S** Attack, ComputerSweden, Corporate Computing, Macworld, Mikrodatorn, Natverk & Kommunikation, PC World, CAP & Design, DataIngenjoren, Maxi Data,Windows World; **SWITZERLAND'S** Computerworld Schweiz, Macworld Schweiz, PC Tip; **TAIWAN'S** Computerworld Taiwan, PC World Taiwan; **THAILAND'S** Thai Computerworld; **TURKEY'S** Computerworld Monitor, Macworld Turkiye, PC World Turkiye; **UKRAINE'S** Computerworld, Computers+Software Magazine; **UNITED KINGDOM'S** Computing /Computerworld, Connexion/Network World, Lotus Magazine, Macworld, Open Computing/Sunworld; **UNITED STATES'** Advanced Systems, AmigaWorld, Cable in the Classroom, CD Review, CIO, Computerworld, Computerworld Client/Server Journal, Digital Video, DOS World, Electronic Entertainment Magazine (E2), Federal Computer Week, Game Hits, GamePro, IDG Books, Infoworld, Laser Event, Macworld, Maximize, Multimedia World, Network World, PC Letter, PC World, Publish, SWATPro, Video Event; **URUGUAY'S** PC World Uruguay; **VENEZUELA'S** Computerworld Venezuela, PC World; **VIETNAM'S** PC World Vietnam. 02/28/95

Acknowledgments

Thank you from the bottom of my heart to all the folks at IDG Books whose hard work and talent helped make this book a reality.

(The publisher would like to thank Patrick J. McGovern, without whom this book would not have been possible.)

Credits

Executive Vice President, Strategic Product Planning and Research
David Solomon

Editorial Director
Diane Graves Steele

Acquisitions Editor
Megg Bonar

Brand Manager
Judith A. Taylor

Editorial Managers
Tracy L. Barr
Sandra Blackthorn
Kristin A. Cocks

Editorial Assistants
Tamara S. Castleman
Stacey Holden Prince
Kevin Spencer

Acquisitions Assistant
Suki Gear

Production Director
Beth Jenkins

Supervisor of Project Coordination
Cindy L. Phipps

Project Coordinator
Valery Bourke

Pre-Press Coordinator
Steve Peake

Associate Pre-Press Coordinator
Tony Augsburger

Project Editor
Julie King

Technical Reviewer
Ben Barbante

Production Staff
Paul Belcastro
Cameron Booker
Linda Boyer
Maridee Ennis
Carla C. Radzikinas
Dwight Ramsey
Patricia R. Reynolds
Gina Scott

Proofreader
Charles A. Hutchinson

Indexer
Nancy Anderman Guenther

Cover Design
Kavish + Kavish

Contents at a Glance

Introduction

This is my third book about Photoshop. The other two, *Photoshop 3 For Macs For Dummies* and *Macworld Photoshop 3 Bible,* approach the topic according to tasks. If you want to accomplish Result A, do Operation B.

This book takes exactly the opposite approach. Rather than explain why things work or how to put them into use, I tell you what Photoshop's tools, palette, commands, and options do. Every single Photoshop function is covered, regardless of how simple or how complex. I also include every keyboard equivalent and every operating tip. If it's in Photoshop, it's in here.

The result is a Photoshop reference guide designed to provide you with a lightning-fast tour through the nuts and bolts of this vast and amazing program. The text is short, sweet, and to the point. It's the next best thing to an intravenous injection of pure, unmitigated information.

How is this book organized?

The book is divided into three basic parts:

- The first part explains everything about the toolbox, including tools, color controls, quick mask icons, and screen modes.
- The second section explains the palettes, which let you create and organize brushes, channels, colors, keyboard shortcuts, layers, and paths.
- The last section explains every one of the commands under the Edit, File, Filter, Image, Mode, Select, and Window menus. I also include figures demonstrating Photoshop's blurring, sharpening, and distortion filters.

All entries are organized alphabetically. In Part I, for example, I discuss the eraser tool before the zoom tool, even though the zoom tool precedes the eraser in the toolbox. Some tools are grouped together. The marquee, lasso, and magic wand tools, for example, are all discussed in "The Selection Tools." It's all pretty straightforward and logical, but if you have problems finding information about a topic, consult the index.

Where do I go from here?

This book is not intended to serve as your one-and-only guide to Photoshop. I offer it merely as a reference book to consult when you're trying to remember what some function or other does. If you aren't clear on a concept or you need to gain a broader understanding of channels, layers, or some other complex topic, please consult *Photoshop 3 For Macs For Dummies* or *Macworld Photoshop 3 Bible*, both of which are self-contained and — I hope — thoroughly readable titles.

The cast of icons

This book uses two sets of icons. One set accompanies the entry titles. The second calls out points of interest in the text.

Each entry appears as white text in a black bar. To the right of the entry name are two icons, one showing whether I recommend the function or not, and a second to let you know how safe it is.

If I recommend a function, I give it the old thumbs up.

If the tool, palette, or command is only occasionally useful, I stamp it with the double-thumb. It's half good, half bad. I'll let you decide whether you want to use it or not.

If I recommend that you steer the heck clear of a function, I curse it with the thumbs-down symbol. I also steer you to the better tool or command so that you aren't left without alternatives.

No matter how you use a function marked with the safe icon, you can't do any damage to your image.

A tool, palette, or command that bears the safety pin icon can cause a small amount of damage if you don't use it correctly.

The skull and crossbones highlights a function that can do serious damage to your image if you're not careful. Frequently, I give an entry both the thumbs up and the skull. This means that the function is very important, but you should use it with care.

The remaining, smaller icons appear in the page margins, just to the left of a noteworthy paragraph of text. If you're fairly experienced with Photoshop, just peruse these icons and ignore the other stuff. These choice nuggets alone should be worth the price of admission.

Here's how to access the function from the keyboard.

This icon marks a highly useful tip that you should immediately integrate into your daily working ritual.

If I want something to stick in your mind, I stamp it with this icon.

Very little about Photoshop is dangerous, but every once in a while, you'll want to keep your guard up.

I can't explain everything in a book that's roughly the size of a woman's wallet. So I've included cross-references to *Photoshop 3 For Macs For Dummies* throughout this book. Check out the chapters indicated for a more insightful, more amusing look at some of Photoshop's more exciting capabilities.

Part I

The Photoshop Toolbox

Basic Toolbox Stuff

The toolbox resides in the upper left corner of the screen. It contains a total of 20 tools (plus four hidden ones). A handful of color controls and additional icons occupy the bottom third of the toolbox.

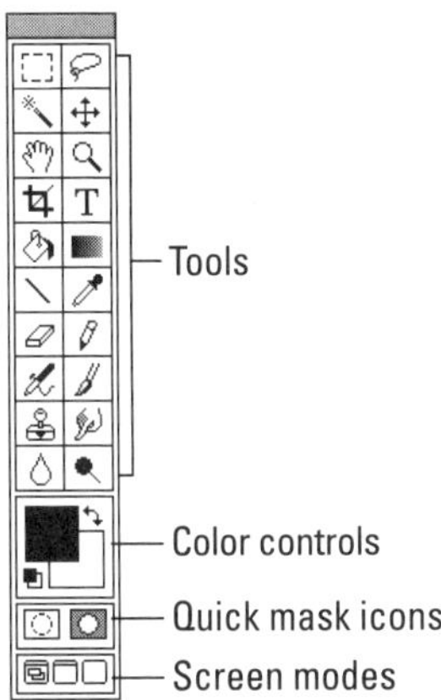

Toolbox Element	*How It Works*
Tools	Tools let you change the appearance of the open image. To use a tool, you must first select it by clicking on its icon in the toolbox (or by pressing the tool's shortcut key). Then click or drag with the tool inside the image window to modify the image.
	To adjust the way a tool works, select the tool icon and press the Return key. This displays the Options palette. Unlike controls in other Photoshop palettes (described in Part II), controls inside the Options palette change to suit the selected tool.

(continued)

Toolbox Element	How It Works
Color controls	Click on one of these icons to change the foreground and/or background colors, which determine the colors applied with the painting and editing tools.
Quick mask icons	The quick mask mode lets you edit selection outlines as if they were stencils. You enter the quick mask mode by clicking on the right icon (or by pressing Q). You return to the standard mode by clicking on the left icon (or pressing Q again). See "Quick Mask Icons" later in Part I for more information.
Screen modes	Click on one of these icons (or press the F key) to change how the image fills the screen. These icons are explained in the "Screen Modes" section later in Part I.

You can hide the toolbox by pressing the Tab key. This also has the effect of hiding all the palettes. If you want to hide just the toolbox but leave the palettes on-screen, press Option-Tab.

Press Tab or Option-Tab again to bring the toolbox and/or palettes back up on-screen.

The Color Controls

Photoshop gives you access to exactly 16,777,216 colors that you can use in your image. Every one of these colors is unique.

To simplify things a little, Photoshop makes two colors active at any one time. These are the foreground and background colors.

Color	What It Does
Foreground color	This color affects the type tool, the paint bucket, the gradient tool, the line tool, the painting tools, and the smudge tool when you are finger painting.

Color	What It Does
Background color	The eraser paints in the background color. The gradient tool fades gradations from the foreground color to the background color. You can also set the Fade option for the painting tools to fade to the background color.

The foreground and background colors are shown in the toolbox.

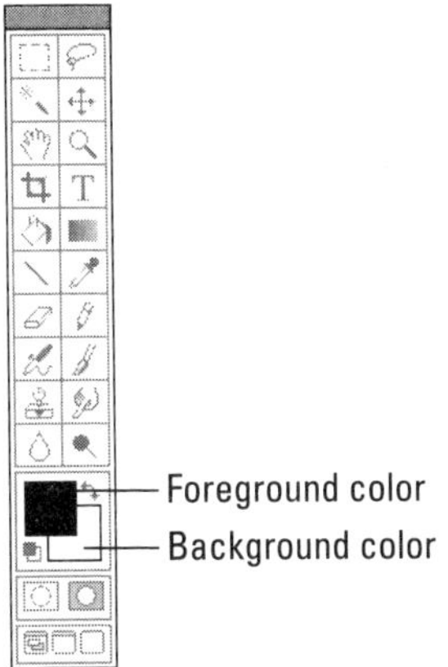

Changing the foreground or background color

When you first start Photoshop, the foreground color is black and the background color is white. You can change either color to any of the other 16 million (or so) colors in any of the following ways:

- Click in the image with the eyedropper tool to change the foreground color to the color you click on. Option-click to change the background color. Both options are described in "The Eyedropper Tool," found later in Part I.
- Take advantage of one of the three color palettes, described in "The Color Palettes" in Part II.
- Click on the foreground or background color icon to display the Color Picker dialog box, which is described two sentences from now.

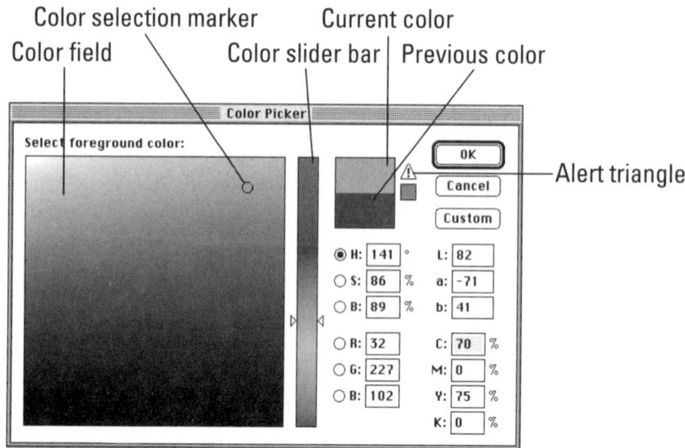

The Color Picker is Photoshop's built-in color laboratory. Here's how it works:

Color Picker Option	***What It Does***
Color field	The color field shows two variations on a color. By default, you see variations on the saturation and brightness of the color, but the hue remains the same throughout.
Color selection marker	Click in the color field to change the location of the circular color selection marker. The color inside the marker becomes the new color.
Color slider bar	The slider bar provides the third variation on the color. By default, you change the hue using the slider, from red at the top to blue, green, yellow, and back to red at the bottom. Drag the slider triangles to pick a new hue.
Current color	This rectangle shows the most recent color you've picked.
Previous color	The rectangle below it shows the color as it appeared before you entered the Color Picker dialog box. Click on this color to restore it.

Color Picker Option	What It Does
Alert triangle	If a color can be displayed on-screen but it cannot be printed — as is common with vivid colors — a little triangle with an exclamation point appears. Below the triangle is a color square that shows the closest printable color. Click on either the triangle or the color square to pick the printable color.
Custom button	Click on the Custom button to access predefined libraries of colors from Pantone, Trumatch, and others.
Cancel button	Click on this button to exit the dialog box and leave the foreground or background color unchanged. KEY SHORTCUT You can also press ⌘-period or Escape to cancel the Color Picker.
OK button	To exit the dialog box and change the color to your new pick, click on the OK button. KEY SHORTCUT Press Return or Enter to activate the OK button from the keyboard.

Using color models

There are four sets of option boxes in the Color Picker dialog box, each of which represents a different model for defining color. Each color model exists independently of the other. They are provided as alternatives to each other. You can use any one of them or rely exclusively on the options discussed in the preceding list.

- H, S, and B stand for hue, saturation, and brightness. Hue is measured on a 360-degree circle, with 0 being red, 120 being green, and 240 being blue. Saturation and brightness are measured in percentages.

  (Brightness is related to luminosity but is slightly different. A B value of 0 percent is black; 50 percent is medium color; and 100 percent is white.)

- R, G, and B stand for red, green, and blue, which are the primary colors of light. Each is measured from 0 to 255 — from no color to full-intensity color. The higher the value, the lighter the color gets.

- The L in the Lab option stands for luminosity; *a* and *b* don't stand for anything. The Lab color model is a theoretical model used to define every color your eye can see.

  Many Lab colors can't be displayed on your monitor; others can't be printed. I have yet to meet anyone who knows the Lab model well enough to enter numerical values and get predictable results, so don't sweat it.
- C, M, Y, and K stand for cyan, magenta, yellow, and black, the four primary colors for commercial printing. Each value can vary from 0 to 100 percent. Higher values result in darker colors, just the opposite of RGB.

The radio buttons next to the HSB and RGB option boxes affect the contents of the color field and slider bar. Select the radio button for the color variable you want to adjust in the slider bar; the other two radio buttons within that color model become variables in the color field.

So if you select R, the slider bar shows what happens when you change the amount of red in a color; the color field shows what happens when you change green and blue.

More color control stuff

In addition to the foreground and background color icons, Photoshop offers two other extremely useful color control icons.

Color Control Icon	How You Use It
Swap colors	Click on this icon to swap the foreground and background colors. You can press X to activate the swap colors icon from the keyboard.
Default colors	Click on this icon to restore black as the foreground color and white as the background color. Press D to get the default colors of black and white.

The Crop Tool

Use the crop tool to clip an image down to a smaller size. For example, you can crop a full body shot so all that's left is the head.

In clipping away unwanted detail, the crop tool throws away pixels from the original image. So for Pete's sake, make sure that you really want to toss that part of your image.

Press C to select the crop tool from the keyboard.

Using the crop tool

1. With the crop tool selected, drag around the portion of the image you want to retain.
2. Adjust the crop boundary by dragging any of the four corner handles.

3. If you want to rotate the crop boundary to correct the slant of an image, Option-drag a corner handle.
4. You can move the crop boundary without changing its size by ⌘-dragging a corner handle.
5. Click inside the crop boundary with the gavel cursor to clip away the unwanted detail.

If you change your mind and decide to cancel the operation, click outside the crop boundary with the cancel cursor, which looks like a circle with a line through it.

Cropping one image to match another

The crop tool has a hidden capability that lets you match one image so that it exactly matches the size of another. This is an important first step if you plan to combine two images using Image⇨Apply Image or Image⇨Calculations.

1. Select the crop tool and press the Return key to display the Cropping Tool Options palette.
2. Select the Fixed Target Size check box in the palette.
3. Click on the title bar of the image whose size you want to match. This brings the image — which I'll call Image A — to the foreground.

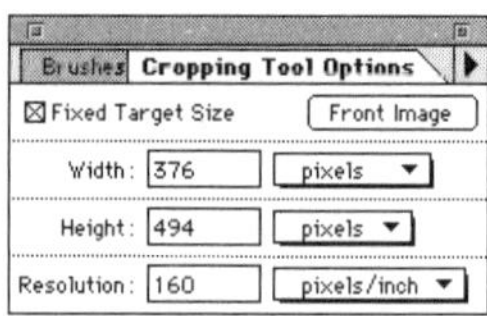

4. Click on the Front Image button in the Cropping Tool Options palette. Photoshop loads the width, height, and resolution of Image A into the Width, Height, and Resolution option boxes.
5. Click on the title bar of the image you want to crop to the new size. Now this image — Image B — is in the foreground.
6. Drag with the crop tool inside Image B. Then modify the crop boundary as desired.

   As you drag, Photoshop constrains the width and height of the crop boundary to match the proportions of Image A.
7. Click inside the crop boundary with the gavel cursor. Photoshop automatically resizes Image B to exactly match the width, height, and resolution of Image A.

The Eraser Tool

You can perform three functions with the eraser tool:

- Drag in the image window on the Background layer to paint with the background color. By default, the background color is white, so this produces the effect of erasing paint away from white paper.
- Drag in a layer other than Background to paint transparent holes into the layer. In other words, you erase portions of the layer to reveal the layers behind it.

If the eraser paints in the background color on a layer, it's because the Preserve Transparency check box is selected in the Layers palette (as described in "The Layers Palette" in Part II). Turn this option off to erase to transparency.

- Option-drag to reveal the image as it appeared when last saved to disk. This way, you can experiment with modifications to your image with the knowledge that you can always return to the saved image simply by erasing.

Photoshop displays an error message if you've changed the size of the image, the color mode, or the blend mode assigned to a layer since it was last saved. You won't be able to Option-drag with the eraser until you restore the old size, color mode, or blend mode.

Press E to select the eraser tool.

Changing how the eraser works

If you're used to using the eraser in the previous version of Photoshop, you'll be happy to know that you are no longer limited to a boxy, hard-edged eraser cursor. In fact, you now have a great deal of control over this tool.

1. Select the eraser tool and press Return to display the Eraser Options palette.

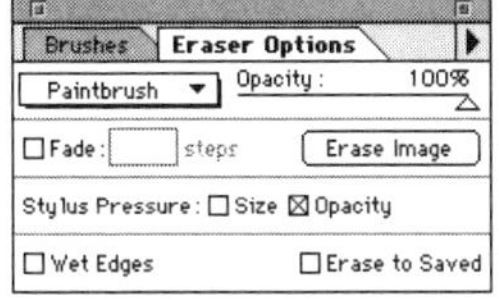

2. Select the type of eraser you want to use from the pop-up menu in the upper left corner of the palette. You can erase with the equivalent of the paintbrush, pencil, or airbrush tools, described in the section "The Painting Tools: Pencil, Airbrush, and Paintbrush" later in Part I. You can also access the old-style boxy eraser by selecting the Block option.

   You can also cycle through the four kinds of erasers by pressing E. Each press of E advances to the next kind of eraser listed in the pop-up menu.

3. Change the Opacity value to paint translucent strokes with the eraser. For example, if you Option-drag with the eraser when the Opacity is lower than 100 percent, you partially reveal the saved image without entirely erasing your changes.

You can change the Opacity from the keyboard when the eraser tool is selected by pressing the number keys. Press 1 for 10 percent, 2 for 20 percent, and so on, up to 0 for 100 percent.

4. When using the paintbrush-style eraser, you can select the Wet Edges check box to change the standard paintbrush to a watercolor brush. The result is an eraser with opaque edges and a translucent center.

   If you can imagine erasing with watercolors, you have a picture of how this option works. You also have a very good imagination.

5. If you use the eraser tool primarily for revealing portions of the saved image, select the Erase to Saved check box to set the eraser to reveal the saved image any time you drag.

   When Erase to Saved is checked, you have to Option-drag to erase to the background color or to transparency on a layer.

6. Click on the Erase Image button to fill the entire image with the background color.

   When you're working on a layer, the button is labeled Erase Layer. Click on this button to make the active layer transparent (unless Preserve Transparency is selected in the Layers palette, in which case Photoshop fills the opaque portion of the layer with the background color).

For more information about layers, see "The Layers Palette" in Part II of this book. To learn how to establish and use layers, check out Chapter 18 in *Photoshop 3 For Macs For Dummies.*

Creating fading strokes

The Eraser Options palette offers two options — Fade and Stylus Pressure — that you also find throughout the Options palettes for the painting tools. It's unlikely you'll have much cause to use these options, but I wouldn't want to deprive you of knowing how they work.

The Fade option lets you erase in a fading stroke. Though the concept is simple, you need some background information to understand how the option works. See, a stroke painted with the eraser — or a painting or editing tool for that matter — may look even and continuous. But the stroke is actually a bunch of round dollops spaced very tightly together.

To fade out an eraser stroke, you first select the Fade check box. Then you enter the number of dollops over which the fade occurs into the option box. As you erase, Photoshop makes each dollop more translucent. By the last dollop, the stroke has completely faded.

Working with a pressure-sensitive tablet

The Stylus Pressure options are dimmed unless you have a pressure-sensitive drawing tablet — such as the Wacom Artpad — hooked up to your computer. If you do have such a tablet, these options let you specify how you want Photoshop to interpret the pressure.

Select the Size option to tell Photoshop to change the thickness of the stroke as you press harder or let up with the stylus. Select Opacity to make the eraser stroke translucent as you lift the stylus.

More eraser tool stuff

You can erase in straight lines by clicking at one location and Shift-clicking at another. Photoshop draws a straight eraser stroke between the two points. Keep Shift-clicking to add more straight strokes.

Another interesting item to keep in mind: If a portion of the image is selected, the eraser works only inside the selection. Deselected portions of the image are not affected.

You can paint inside selections and Shift-click to create straight lines with all painting and editing tools. These include the pencil, paintbrush, airbrush, rubber stamp, smudge, focus, and toning tools.

The Eyedropper Tool

The eyedropper tool lets you “lift” colors from the image. Click on a color in the image to make that color the foreground color. For example, if you click in a blue sky, the foreground color becomes blue.

Option-click with the eyedropper tool to change the background color.

You can get the eyedropper tool when the paint bucket, gradient, line, paintbrush, pencil, or airbrush tool is selected by pressing and holding the Option key. Option-click in the image with one of these tools to change the foreground color.

Better yet, select the eyedropper from the keyboard by pressing the I key. The I key works no matter which tool is selected, and you can change either the foreground or background color.

Changing the sample size

When you click with the eyedropper tool, you lift the color from the exact pixel on which you click. But you can tell Photoshop to blend neighboring pixels to get an average color.

1. Select the eyedropper tool and press Return to display the Eyedropper Options palette.

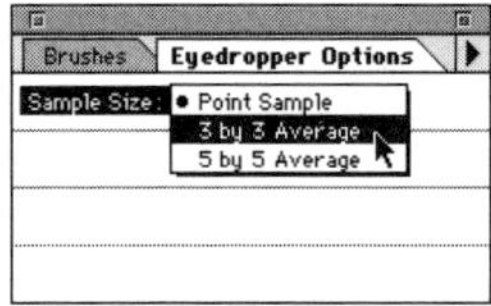

2. Select an option from the Sample Size pop-up menu.
   - Select Point Sample to take the color from the single pixel on which you click.
   - The 3 by 3 Average option averages the colors of the pixel on which you click with its eight immediate neighbors.
   - Select 5 by 5 Average to average the colors of the closest 25 pixels.

Changing the Sample Size setting also affects the sensitivity of the magic wand tool. So if you notice the magic wand behaving strangely, set the Sample Size option back to Point Sample.

The Fill Tools: Paint Bucket and Gradient

Photoshop provides two tools for filling areas with color.

Fill Tool	*How You Use It*
 Paint bucket	Click inside an area of color to fill that area with the foreground color. For example, if the foreground color were red, you could click in a blue sky to fill the sky with red without affecting the clouds.
	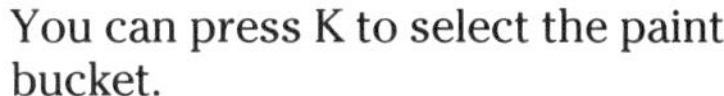 You can press K to select the paint bucket.
 Gradient	Drag inside a selection to fill the selection with a gradation that starts with the foreground color and ends with the background color.
	The point where you start dragging determines the location of the foreground color; the point where you release positions the background color. The direction of the drag determines the direction of the gradient.
	Press G to select the gradient fill tool.

Changing how the paint bucket works

The paint bucket is a coloring tool with a built-in magic wand function. In fact, it relies on the very same sensitivity options as the magic wand, Tolerance and Anti-aliased. (The magic wand is discussed later in Part I, in the section "The Selection Tools: Marquee, Lasso, and Magic Wand.") The following steps show you how to modify the performance of the tool. With the exception of the first step, all the others are optional, so you can perform them in any order you please.

1. Select the paint bucket tool and press the Return key to display the Paint Bucket Options palette.

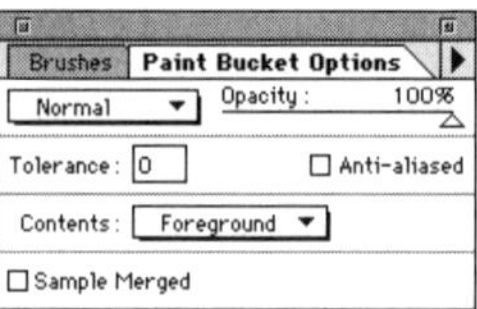

2. Adjust the Tolerance value to change the size of the area affected by the paint bucket. The Tolerance value determines how similar colors have to be for the paint bucket to affect them, much as it does for the magic wand. The higher the number, the more colors the tool affects.
3. To fill an area without softening the edges, turn off the Anti-aliased check box.
4. Select the Sample Merged check box to fill pixels on the active layer based on the colors of pixels on other layers.

   Suppose that you have a blue sky on one layer — call it Layer 1 — but the layer above it — Layer 2 — is active. With Sample Merged turned on, you can click in Layer 2 to fill the area in front of the blue sky with red. Meanwhile, the blue sky remains intact, just in case you want to retrieve it later.
5. You can fill an area either with the foreground color or with a pattern created by choosing Edit➪Define Pattern (as explained in Part III). To choose between foreground color or pattern, select an option from the Contents pop-up menu.
6. To mix the foreground color (or pattern) with the existing colors in the image, change the Opacity value. A value of 100 percent fills the area with the foreground color exclusively. A value of 50 percent mixes foreground color and existing colors in equal amounts.

You can change the Opacity value from the keyboard by pressing number keys. Press 1 for 10 percent, 2 for 20 percent, and so on, up to 0 for 100 percent.

7. Select an option from the pop-up menu in the upper left corner of the Paint Bucket Options palette to change the method Photoshop uses to blend the foreground color (or pattern) with the existing colors in the image. Called *blend modes* or — in some rarefied circles — *calculations*, these options are among the most exciting functions in Photoshop.

Selecting a blend mode

Blend modes let you mix colors in different ways. Suppose that you want to make the sky in your image red. But you don't want to fill the sky with flat red; you just want to change the color of the sky to red and leave the highlights and shadows intact. To color the sky, you select the Color blend mode from the pop-up menu before clicking with the paint bucket tool.

Here's how the blend modes work:

Blend Mode	*How It Works*
Normal	The default mode, Normal fills a colored region with the flat foreground color.
Dissolve	Dissolve fringes the antialiased edges of the filled area with a random scatter of pixels, creating a roughened effect.
Behind	When working on a layer other than Background, select this blend mode to fill the transparent area behind the layer without affecting opaque pixels on the layer.
Clear	Again, this option works only when you are editing a layer. Clear fills an area with transparency, regardless of the foreground color. So it's like filling an area with a hole.
Multiply	Multiply darkens existing colors, as if the foreground color were ink spilled from a bottle. Some folks think of it as a magic marker effect. Use it with light and medium colors. (It has no effect on black.)

(continued)

Blend Mode	How It Works
Screen	The exact opposite of Multiply, Screen lightens colors as if the foreground color were a light cast on the image. Use this mode with dark colors. (It has no effect on white.)
Overlay	This mode mixes the foreground color with the existing colors in the image in fairly even increments, darkening or lightening the image only if the foreground color is darker or lighter than the existing colors.
Soft Light	A wimpy version of Overlay, Soft Light casts a soft glazing of foreground color over the image.
Hard Light	Hard Light is the opposite of Overlay, which means that it favors the foreground color over the existing colors in the image. Use it when you want an effect somewhere between Normal and Overlay.
Darken	When you select Darken, the paint bucket fills an area only if the foreground color is darker than the existing pixels in the image. Otherwise, the existing pixels remain unaffected.
Lighten	When you select Lighten, the paint bucket fills an area only if the foreground color is lighter than the existing pixels.
Difference	Difference inverts the image according to the foreground color. A dark foreground color has little effect, but a light foreground color turns the image into a photo-negative.
Hue	The Hue blend mode applies the hue of the foreground color but retains the saturation and luminosity of the original image.
Saturation	Saturation applies the saturation of the foreground color to the hues and luminosities in the image. It's useful for boosting colors or fading them.

Blend Mode	How It Works
Color	This mode applies both the hue and saturation of the foreground color but keeps the luminosity of the original image. It's one of my favorite modes to use with the paint bucket tool.
Luminosity	This option leaves the hues and saturation levels of the image unscathed and applies the luminosity of the foreground color. This allows you to lighten or darken colors uniformly.

The three properties of color are hue (the pure color), saturation (how vivid or gray the color is), and luminosity (its lightness or darkness). These three properties correspond respectively to the Tint, Color, and Brightness knobs on a TV.

You can combine any of the blend modes with different Opacity settings, making it possible to apply literally thousands of variations with a single foreground color. These same blend modes are available when you use the gradient, line, paintbrush, pencil, airbrush, and rubber stamp tools. (Only the paint bucket and line tool offer the Clear mode. The eraser takes over this purpose from the other tools.)

Chapter 8 in *Photoshop 3 For Macs For Dummies* shows some specific ways to use the Multiply, Screen, Overlay, and Difference modes with the paintbrush, airbrush, and pencil tools.

Changing how the gradient fill tool works

You can create two basic kinds of gradations with the gradient tool — linear, which progresses directly from the foreground color to the background color, and radial, which progresses outward in concentric circles. Here's how to change how the gradient tool works:

1. Select the gradient tool and press the Return key to display the Gradient Tool Options palette.

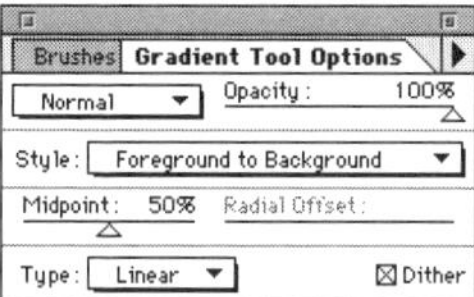

2. Select whether you want to create a Linear or Radial gradation from the Type pop-up menu (at the bottom of the palette).
3. Adjust the Midpoint slider to change where the medium color between the foreground and background colors appears in the gradation. Lower the slider value to emphasize the background color; raise the slider value to emphasize the foreground color.
4. When you're creating a Radial gradation, the Radial Offset slider lets you increase the size of the inner circle of foreground color. Normally, the value is set to 0 percent, so the foreground color is just a pinpoint in the center.
5. The Style pop-up menu lets you specify the colors that appear in the gradation.
   - Foreground to Background blends between the foreground and background colors.
   - If you select one of the Transparent options, the gradient tool blends the foreground color into the original colors in the image. Foreground to Transparent places the foreground color at the beginning of the gradation; Transparent to Foreground places it at the end, which you might find helpful when creating radial gradations.
   - The two Spectrum options apply to full-color gradients only, creating a rainbow of colors between the foreground and background colors. Clockwise Spectrum goes one direction around the rainbow; Counterclockwise Spectrum goes the other way. Experiment to see which one best suits your needs.
6. The Dither check box randomizes the gradient to make it print smoother. Leave it selected.
7. Adjust the Opacity value to make the gradient translucent. As you can with the paint bucket, you can change this value from the keyboard by pressing a number key when the gradient tool is selected. Press 1 for 10 percent, 2 for 20 percent, and so on, up to 0 for 100 percent.
8. To change the way Photoshop mixes colors from the gradation with those in the original image, select one of the blend modes described in "Selecting a blend mode" earlier in this section.

The Focus Tools: Blur and Sharpen

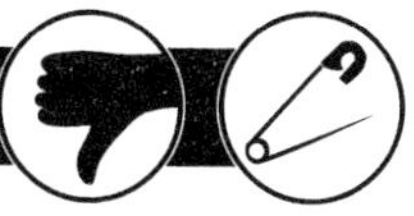

The bottom left tool slot in the toolbox houses two focus tools, which you use to blur or sharpen the focus of the image.

Focus Tool	How You Use It
Blur	Drag in the image to blur pixels. This tool softens harsh edges and smoothes out rough transitions.
	Press R to select the blur tool.
Sharpen	Drag to increase the contrast between pixels, producing the effect of sharper focus.
	If the blur tool is selected, press R again to select the sharpen tool.

You can also Option-drag with either tool to produce the effect of the other. Option-dragging with the blur tool, for example, sharpens.

Personally, I don't care for either of these tools because they provide so little control. If you want to blur and sharpen pixels, I recommend that you select the area you want to change and apply the commands under the Filter⇨Blur and Filter⇨Sharpen submenus (as described in Part III).

Changing how the focus tools work

1. Select the blur or sharpen tool and press Return to display the Focus Tools Options palette.

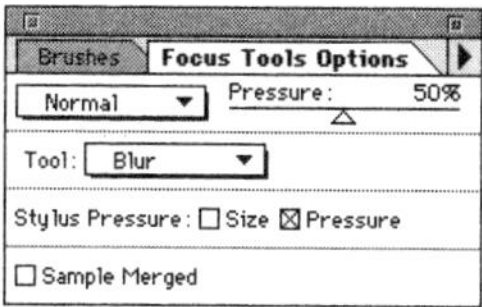

2. Select the type of focus tool you want to use — Blur or Sharpen — from the Tool pop-up menu.
3. Adjust the Pressure slider bar setting to control the impact of the tool. Higher percentages blur or sharpen image details more dramatically.

   As always, you can change the Pressure setting from the keyboard by pressing number keys. Press 1 for 10 percent, 2 for 20 percent, and so on, up to 0 for 100 percent.
4. Select the Sample Merged check box to blur or sharpen details from other layers onto the active layer.
5. The blend modes work just like they do with the eraser, painting, and rubber stamp tools, except that there are fewer of them. Like the smudge tool, the focus tools offer only seven modes, Normal, Darken, Lighten, Hue, Saturation, Color, and Luminosity.

   See the "Selecting a blend mode" section of "The Fill Tools: Paint Bucket and Gradient" earlier in Part I for information about how the modes work.
6. Use the Stylus Pressure check boxes as described earlier in the "Working with a pressure-sensitive tablet" section of "The Eraser Tool."

The Line Tool

Drag with the line tool to add straight lines to your image. The point at which you start dragging determines the starting point in the line; the point at which you release determines the end point.

To select the line tool from the keyboard, press N.

It's usually easier to create straight lines by Shift-clicking with the painting tools or paint outlines around selections by choosing Edit⇨Stroke (as explained in Part III) than it is to use the line tool. The line tool is great for making arrows, however, as explained next.

Making arrows

The line tool is most useful for creating arrows — something you can't do using any other function inside Photoshop.

Here's how to set up arrows:

1. Select the line tool and press Return to highlight the Line Width value inside the Line Tool Options palette.
2. Enter the thickness of the line you want to draw into the Line Width option box.

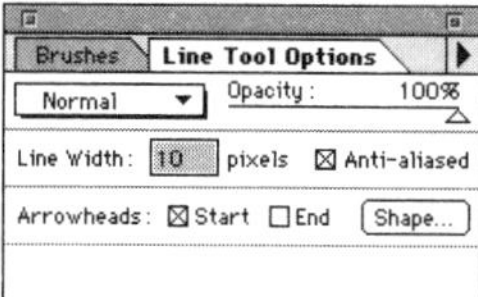

3. Select the Start or End check box to attach the arrowhead to the start or end of the line. To create a line with two arrowheads, select both options.
4. Click on the Shape button to define what the arrowhead looks like. A dialog box comes up, offering three options, Width, Length, and Concavity:
   - The Width value controls the width of the arrowhead, measured as a percentage of the thickness of the line. So if the line is 10 pixels thick and the Width value is set to 500 percent, the arrowhead will be 50 pixels wide.
   - The Length value determines the length of the arrowhead, again measured as a percentage of the line thickness.
   - The Concavity value determines the curvature of the base of the arrowhead. (The base is the side that meets with the line.) Positive values curve the base inward; negative values curve it outward.

More line tool stuff

By default, Photoshop softens the edges of lines using antialiasing. To create hard-edged lines, turn off the Anti-aliased check box in the Line Tool Options palette.

To draw lines that are exactly vertical or horizontal, Shift-drag with the line tool. You can also create pre cisely diagonal lines at a 45-degree angle.

You can also apply Opacity values and blend modes to lines drawn with the line tool, as described back in the "Selecting a blend mode" section of "The Fill Tools: Paint Bucket and Gradient" earlier in Part I.

The Move Tool

The move tool lets you move portions of an image. It isn't the only method for moving image elements, of course. You can move a selection by simply dragging it with one of the three selection tools. But the move tool provides a couple of unique advantages:

- You can move a selected area of an image by dragging with the move tool anywhere inside the image window. This option is great for moving partially selected areas or complex selections that are hard to grab hold of.
- When nothing is selected, you can move the entire active layer by dragging in the image window.
- If you drag a deselected image from one image window to another open image window, Photoshop automatically places the moved image on its own layer.

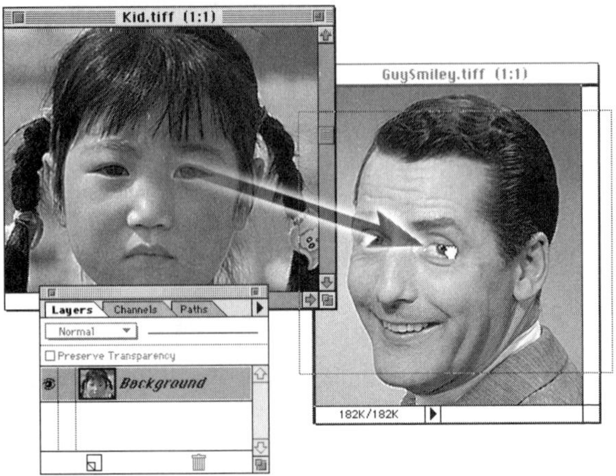

5. Change the blend mode and Opacity settings as desired. These work as described earlier in "The Fill Tools: Paint Bucket and Gradient."

6. If you have a pressure-sensitive tablet, you may want to change the Stylus Pressure settings. I explained these earlier in the "Working with a pressure-sensitive tablet" section of "The Eraser Tool."

7. To clone pixels from inactive layers onto the active layer, select the Sample Merged check box. Otherwise, you can only clone portions of the active layer, many of which may be transparent.

The Sample Merged check box affects cloning only. When the rubber stamp is set to paint patterns or reveal the saved image, the check box is dimmed.

8. Drag in the image window to duplicate portions of the image.

You can clone one image into another. For example, suppose you want to clone parts of Image A into Image B. Option-click in Image A and then drag in Image B.

Painting patterns

You can use the rubber stamp to paint with a pattern that you establish by choosing Edit⇨Define Pattern, as discussed in Part III. The process works basically like cloning, explained earlier in this section, but there are a few differences.

1. Select the rubber stamp tool and press Return to display the Rubber Stamp Options palette.

2. Choose either Pattern (Aligned) or Pattern (Non-Aligned) from the Option pop-up menu.

   - The Pattern (Aligned) option makes sure that the pattern is consistent, no matter how many times you drag with the rubber stamp tool.

   - The Pattern (Non-Aligned) option starts the pattern over again each time you drag with the tool. This results in a more hodgepodge pattern, which may actually look more natural.

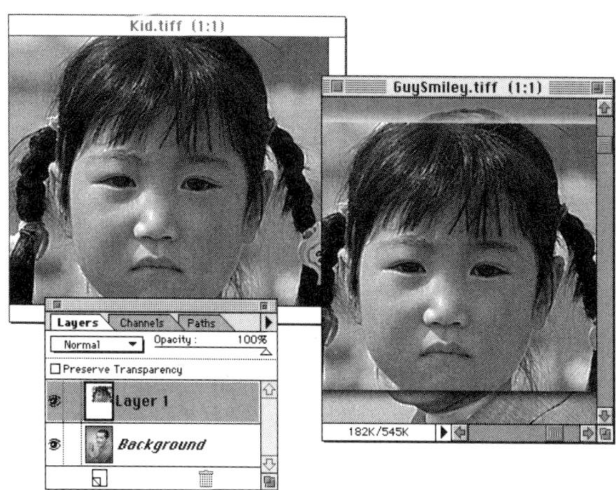

To select the move tool from the keyboard, press V.

The Navigation Tools: Zoom and Hand

The next two tools in the toolbox let you adjust the view of your image. Neither tool changes the image one iota. Rather, these tools allow you to change what you see on-screen.

Navigation Tool	*How You Use It*
 Hand	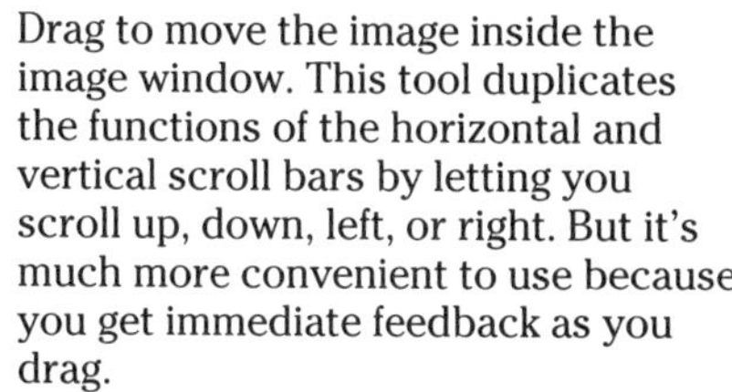 Drag to move the image inside the image window. This tool duplicates the functions of the horizontal and vertical scroll bars by letting you scroll up, down, left, or right. But it's much more convenient to use because you get immediate feedback as you drag.
	To access the hand tool without clicking on its icon, press the spacebar. As long as the spacebar is down, the hand tool remains available.
	To select the hand tool, press H.

(continued)

Navigation Tool	*How You Use It*
Zoom	Click with this tool to magnify the image on-screen. This lets you inspect the image more closely. To reduce the image and take in more of it at a time, Option-click with the zoom tool. You can zoom in when any tool is selected by ⌘-spacebar-clicking. To zoom out, Option-spacebar-click. Or, if you prefer, select the zoom tool by pressing Z.

More zooming stuff

When you zoom, the title bar lists the *zoom ratio* — that is, the number of screen pixels for every image pixel. A zoom ratio of 1:8, for example, means that you can see just one pixel on-screen for every 8 by 8-pixel chunk of image. A zoom ratio of 8:1 means that each image pixel is 8 screen pixels tall and 8 screen pixels wide. So the image is magnified by 800 percent.

The largest zoom ratio is 16:1 and the smallest is 1:16. If you can't zoom in or out any farther, the plus or minus sign inside the magnifying glass cursor disappears.

The following list tells a few special ways to use the zoom tool. As you'll see, even the hand tool can have an effect on the zoom ratio.

Zoom Tool Trick	*What It Does*
Drag in the image window	When you drag in the image window with the zoom tool, you surround a detail with a rectangular marquee. When you release, Photoshop magni fies the marqueed area so that it fills the image window.
Double-click on the zoom icon	This returns the image to the 1:1 zoom ratio. Each and every pixel in the image takes up one screen pixel. This view size is the most accurate, but you may not be able to see the entire image.

Zoom Tool Trick	What It Does
Double-click on the hand icon	This zooms the image so that the entire image fits on-screen or so the image fills the screen. It may reduce or magnify the image depending on the size of the image and the size of your screen.

When the zoom tool is selected, pressing Return brings up the Zoom Tool Options palette. Clicking on the Zoom to Screen button fits the image in the window, just as if you had double-clicked on the hand tool icon in the toolbox. Clicking on the Zoom 1:1 button is the same as double-clicking on the zoom tool icon.

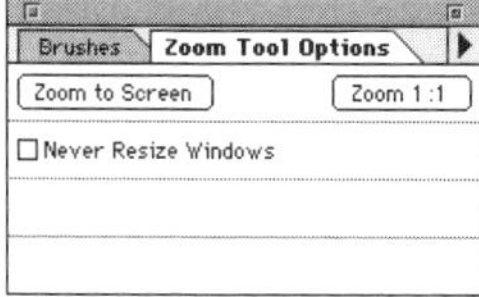

The Never Resize Windows check box affects the Zoom In and Zoom Out commands in the Window menu (see "Window⇨Zoom In" and "Window⇨Zoom Out" in Part III). Normally, these commands resize the image window as they zoom, but you can prevent this from happening by selecting this check box.

For all the information you'd ever want on navigating inside Photoshop, see Chapter 2, "Canvassing the On-Screen Canvas," in *Photoshop 3 For Macs For Dummies*.

The Painting Tools: Pencil, Airbrush, and Paintbrush

Photoshop provides three painting tools that you can use to apply foreground color to an image. You can use these tools to make small edits to an existing image or to paint an original image.

Painting Tool	How You Use It
Pencil	Drag in the image area to paint a hard-edged line in the foreground color. By default, the line is only one pixel thick, but you can change that in the Brushes palette (described in "The Brushes Palette" in Part II).
	Select the pencil by pressing P.
Airbrush	Drag with this tool to paint a very soft stroke that resembles — guess what? — a stroke painted by a traditional airbrush. This is the only painting tool that continually pumps out paint any time the mouse button is down, even when you don't move the cursor.
	Press A to get the airbrush.
Paintbrush	Drag with the paintbrush to paint a smooth stroke. This is the painting tool you'll use most often.
	To select the paintbrush, press B.

Changing how the pencil works

You modify the performance of all the painting tools in basically the same way. So first I'll tell you how to adjust the pencil tool, and then I'll tell you how the two other painting tools differ.

1. Select the pencil tool and press the Return key to display the Pencil Options palette.

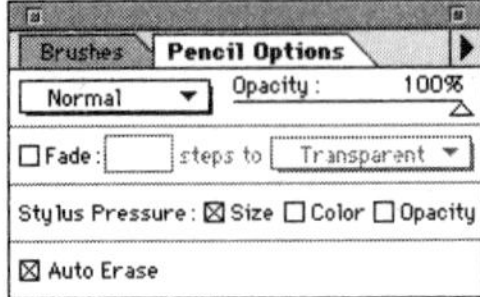

2. Change the Opacity setting to paint with a translucent coating of foreground color. Lower values make your stroke more translucent.
3. To mix the foreground color with the existing pixels in the image in some special way, choose a different option from the modes pop-up menu in the upper left corner of the palette. (I explain how these modes work in the "Selecting a blend mode" section of "The Fill Tools: Paint Bucket and Gradient" earlier in Part I.)
4. Select the Fade option to fade the brushstroke. Enter the number of dollops over which the stroke fades into the option box (as explained earlier in the "Creating fading strokes" section of "The Eraser Tool").
5. You can fade the brushstroke from the foreground color to either transparent or the background color by selecting an option from the pop-up menu to the right of Fade.
6. If you have a pressure-sensitive tablet hooked up to your computer, select one or more Style Pressure check boxes to control how Photoshop interprets the pressure.
   - Select Size to change the thickness of the stroke according to how hard you press on the stylus.
   - The Color check box tells Photoshop to vary the color of the stroke from the foreground color to the background color as you let up on the stylus.
   - If you select Opacity, Photoshop makes the stroke translucent as you lift the stylus.
7. Select the Auto Erase check box to make the pencil perform like pencils in other painting programs. That is, if you click on an area that's already colored in the foreground color, the pencil paints in the background color. Otherwise, it paints with the foreground color.

Changing the airbrush and paintbrush

For the most part, the options inside the Airbrush Options and Paintbrush Options palettes are the same as those inside the Pencil Options palette, described in the preceding paragraphs. The only differences are

- Only the Pencil Options palette offers an Auto Erase check box.
- The Paintbrush Options palette includes a Wet Edges check box. When checked, this option makes the paintbrush paint like a watercolor brush, with opaque edges and a translucent interior.
- In the Airbrush Options palette, the Opacity slider bar is labeled Pressure. Rather than producing translucent strokes at lower settings, the airbrush applies less paint. It's like tightening the nozzle on a real airbrush.
- There are only two Stylus Pressure check boxes, Color and Pressure. The latter varies the Pressure setting as you press harder or let up with the stylus.

Quick Mask Icons

Normally, Photoshop shows selected areas of an image using an animated dot pattern, fancifully known as *marching ants.* You modify the selection outlines using the marquee, lasso, and magic wand tools, as described later in "The Selection Tools: Marquee, Lasso, and Magic Wand."

The quick mask mode offers a different way of looking at selections. When in the quick mask mode, Photoshop shows the selection as a red overlay. Where the overlay is red, the image is not selected; where the overlay is transparent, the image is selected. Soft or blurry edges between red and transparent areas represent antialiased or feathered selections.

In the quick mask mode, you cannot move the selection or otherwise edit it. Rather, you modify the selection outline using painting and editing tools. For example, to enlarge the selected area, you paint with white. To deselect areas, you paint with black.

The two quick mask icons work like so:

Quick Mask Icon	How You Use It
Marching ants	Click on this icon to exit the quick mask mode and return to the standard mode, where selections appear outlined by marching ants.
Quick mask	Click on this icon to enter the quick mask mode. Provided some portion of the image was selected, a red overlay covers the deselected portions of the image. If no portion of the image was selected, the image won't look any different than it looked before. However, you will now be able to paint in the quick mask mode to deselect areas.

You can enter and exit the quick mask mode by pressing Q.

Using the quick mask mode

Because this mode is among the most complex tasks in Photoshop to conceptualize, the following steps explain how to modify a selection outline in the quick mask mode:

1. Use the rectangular marquee tool to select an area in your image, as explained in the upcoming section "The Selection Tools: Marquee, Lasso, and Magic Wand."

2. Press Q to enter the quick mask mode. The area inside the rectangle appears normal, but the deselected area outside the rectangle is coated with red.

3. Press D to change the foreground color to black.
4. Select the paintbrush tool by pressing B.
5. Paint inside the rectangle. In my example, I painted an M. Though the foreground color is black, you paint in red, applying the red coating. The area you paint will become deselected later when you exit the quick mask mode.
6. Press X to swap the foreground and background colors. This makes the foreground color white.
7. Paint outside the rectangle. I painted loops at the corners of my example image. Rather than painting in white, Photoshop erases the red coating. The areas you paint will become selected.

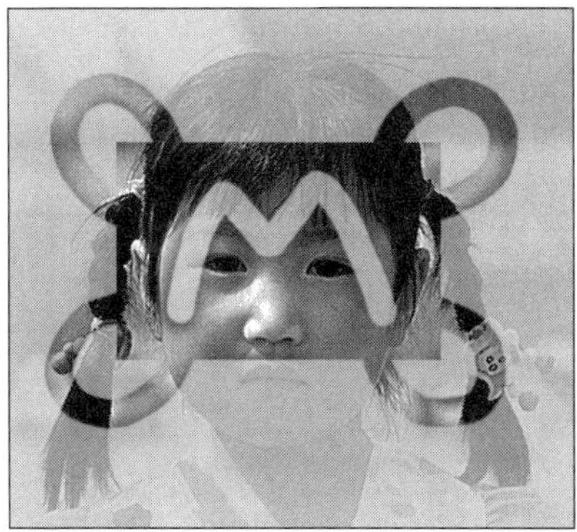

You could alternatively leave the background color set to white and use the eraser tool to create transparent areas in the mask.

8. Press Q to exit the quick mask mode. Now the mask appears as a standard selection outline, complete with marching ants.

Changing the quick mask color

If you're having problems distinguishing the red overlay — for example, maybe there's already a lot of red in your image — you can change the color of the mask.

1. Double-click on either the marching ants or quick mask mode icon. This displays the Quick Mask Options dialog box.

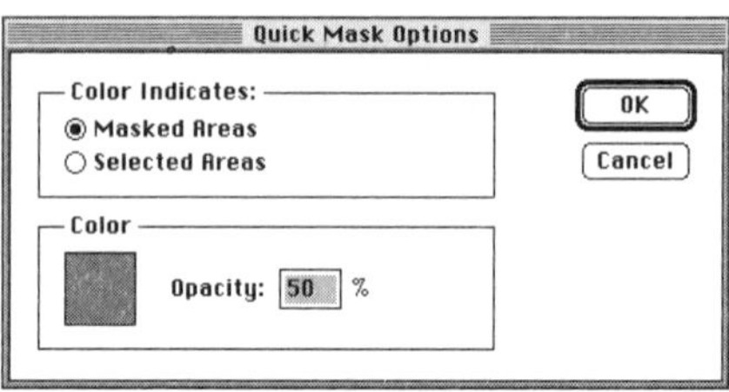

2. The first two radio buttons determine whether the color overlay covers deselected or selected areas. Select the first option, Masked Areas, to cover the deselected areas. Select the second option, Selected Areas, to cover the selected areas.

   You can switch this setting without entering the Quick Mask Options dialog box. Just Option-click on either the marching ants or quick mask icon. The quick mask icon even changes to reflect the new setting.

3. Click on the Color square to bring up the Color Picker dialog box. Select a new color (as described earlier in "The Color Controls") and press Return.
4. Change the value in the Opacity option box to adjust the translucency of the color overlay.
5. Click on the OK button or press Return.

The Rubber Stamp Tool

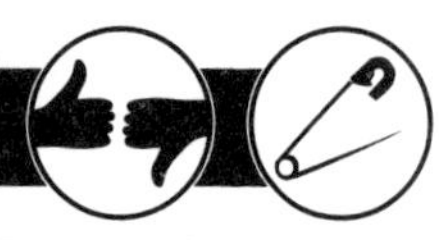

The rubber stamp tool is several tools in one. First and foremost, it's a cloning tool, meaning that you can use it to copy portions of an image onto other portions of an image. This is a wonderful use for the tool.

The other uses are less wonderful. You can paint with a pattern (snore), revert to a previous version of the image (moderately interesting), and create a useless and generally ugly impressionist effect (need I say more).

For some examples of the rubber stamp tool in action, read Chapter 10, "Cleaning Up Goobers," in *Photoshop 3 For Macs For Dummies.*

Press S to select the rubber stamp tool.

Cloning with the rubber stamp

1. Select the rubber stamp tool.
2. Option-click on the portion of the image you want to clone. This sets the clone source.

   Even though nothing seems to happen — Photoshop doesn't say "thank you" or anything — this is a very important step.
3. Press Return to display the Rubber Stamp Options palette.

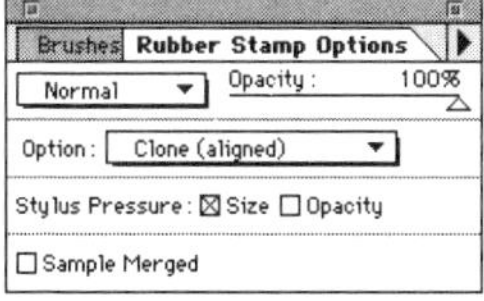

4. Choose either Clone (Aligned) or Clone (Non-Aligned) from the Option pop-up menu in the palette.
   - Choose the Clone (Aligned) option to clone from a relative location. If you move your cursor to a different location, the clone source moves with you.
   - If you want to clone multiple times from a single location, choose Clone (Non-Aligned). This way, you can Option-click once to set the source and then drag multiple times to duplicate that source.

3. Adjust the blend mode, Opacity, and Stylus Pressure settings if you like.
4. Drag with the rubber stamp inside the image window.

Revealing a previous version of the image

When it comes to revealing portions of a stored image, the rubber stamp largely duplicates the effect you get when Option-dragging with the eraser tool. The differences are that the rubber stamp can reveal a snapshot, as described in the upcoming steps, while the eraser reveals only the saved image. Also, you can take advantage of blend modes when using the rubber stamp.

On the other hand, Photoshop provides four different kinds of erasers, and you can apply the Fade option to eraser strokes. So each tool has its own strengths.

To use the rubber stamp tool to revert part of your image to the way it looked in a previous version:

1. Select the rubber stamp tool and press Return to display the Rubber Stamp Options palette.
2. Choose either From Snapshot or From Saved from the Option pop-up menu.
   - Photoshop lets you take a picture of an image and store it in RAM by choosing Edit⇨Take Snapshot (as described in Part III). When you choose the From Snapshot command inside the Rubber Stamp Options palette, the rubber stamp reveals portions of this stored image.
   - Use the From Saved option to reveal portions of the image as it appeared when last saved to disk (with File⇨Save).
3. Mess with the blend mode, Opacity, and Stylus Pressure settings as your conscience directs. (For information on how these settings work, read "The Fill Tools: Paint Bucket and Gradient" and "The Eraser Tool" earlier in Part I.)
4. Drag with the rubber stamp in the image window.

If Photoshop produces an error message, it's because you changed the size of the image, the color mode, or the blend mode assigned to a layer since the image was last saved. Restore the original size, color mode, or blend mode and try again.

Painting an "impressionistic" effect

You can also use the rubber stamp to create an "impressionistic" effect. I put "impressionistic" in quotes because I don't think that the effect looks impressionistic at all. It just looks blurry and uninspired. But it's really up to you to decide.

1. Select the rubber stamp tool and press Return to display the Rubber Stamp Options palette.
2. Choose Impressionist from the Option pop-up menu. This mixes the saved version of the image with the present image and smears it around.
3. The blend mode, Opacity, and Stylus Pressure settings are still in force. Experiment with them to get semi-interesting effects. For more information on these settings, read "The Fill Tools: Paint Bucket and Gradient" and "The Eraser Tool" earlier in Part I.
4. Drag with the rubber stamp in the image window.

Again, you'll get an error message if the size of the image or the active layer's blend mode or color mode has changed since the image was saved.

Screen Modes

The three screen mode icons change how the forward image window fills the screen.

Screen Mode Icon	What It Does
Normal window	Click on the first icon to view the window normally, with scroll bars and title bar and all that stuff. This is the default setting.
Fill screen	Click on this icon to hide the scroll bars and title bar and fill the screen with the image.

Screen Mode Icon	What It Does
	Any portions of the screen that aren't consumed by the image appear gray. The toolbox, palettes, and menu bar remain visible.
Hide menu bar	If you want to take over still more screen real estate, click on the third icon to hide the menu bar. Now any portions of the screen that don't contain an image are filled with black. Only the toolbox and palettes remain visible, and you can hide these by pressing Tab. Press Tab again to redisplay the toolbox and palettes.

Press F to advance from one screen mode to the next. When the menu bar is hidden, pressing F returns to the normal window view.

The Selection Tools: Marquee, Lasso, and Magic Wand

The first three tools in the toolbox let you select the portion of the image that you want to modify. For example, if you want to change the color of a person's face, you first have to isolate the face from the rest of the image by selecting it.

Selection Tool	How You Use It
Rectangular marquee	Drag to select a rectangular portion of the image. The point at which you start dragging determines one corner of the rectangle; the point at which you release the mouse button determines the opposite corner. To select the rectangular marquee tool from the keyboard, press M.
Lasso	Drag to select a free-form area of the image. The better you draw, the better your selection outline looks. Simple tool, hard to master.

(continued)

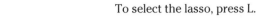

Selection Tool	How You Use It
	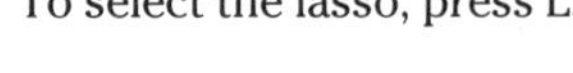 To select the lasso, press L.
	Unlike lassos in other painting programs — which select the colored portions of the image without selecting the white parts — the one in Photoshop creates a selection outline that conforms to the exact movements of your cursor.
 Magic wand	If you want Photoshop to do the selecting for you, click with the magic wand tool to select an area of continuous color. To select a blue sky without selecting the clouds or the mountains, for example, just click in the sky.
	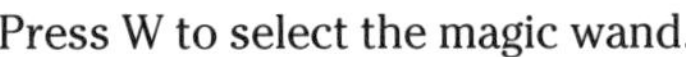 Press W to select the magic wand.

Changing how the marquee works

You can use the rectangular marquee tool right away, or you can modify the way it works by following these steps. All the steps are optional, so after you complete Step 1, you can perform the others in any order you want.

1. Select the marquee tool and press Return to display the Marquee Options palette.

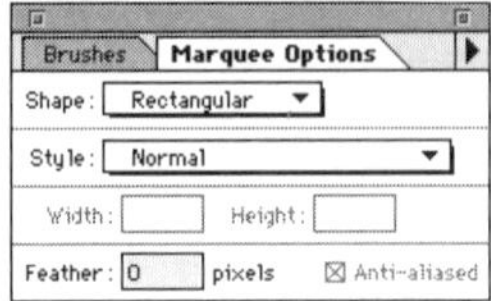

2. Change the shape of the marquee by selecting a different option from the Shape pop-up menu. For example, to create an oval marquee, select the Elliptical option.

   Another way to select the elliptical marquee tool is to press M when the rectangular marquee tool is active. The marquee tool icon in the toolbox changes from rectangular to elliptical. Press M again to return to the rectangular marquee tool.

3. If you want to draw a marquee that is a certain amount wider than it is tall, select the Constrained Aspect Ratio from the Style pop-up menu and enter values in the Width and Height option boxes.
   - For example, to select a rectangular area that is twice as wide as it is tall, enter 2 for the Width value and 1 for Height.
   - To draw a rectangle that is half as wide as it is tall, enter 1 for Width and 2 for Height.
4. If you want to draw a marquee that is a specific size, select the Fixed Size option from the Style pop-up menu and enter the exact size in the Width and Height option boxes.
5. To make the edges of the selection blurry, enter a value into the Feather option box. Higher values result in blurrier edges. A value of 0 creates sharp edges.
6. When the elliptical marquee tool is active, the Anti-aliased check box becomes available. Turn the check box off if you want the oval selection to have *very* sharp edges, which may be jagged. (Usually, you'll want to leave this check box on.)

Any changes made to the options in the Marquee Options palette affect the performance of the marquee tool the very next time you use it. You won't change the shape of the existing selection.

Changing how the lasso works

1. Select the lasso tool and press Return to display the Lasso Options palette.

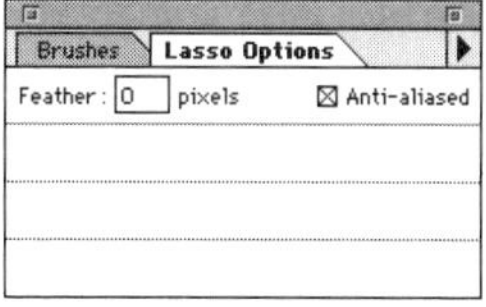

2. Raise the Feather value to give a selection blurry edges.
3. Turn off the Anti-aliased check box to create a selection outline with harsh, abrupt edges. Turn the option on to soften the edges and make them look more naturalistic.

Changing how the magic wand works

1. Select the magic wand and press Return to bring up the Magic Wand Options palette.

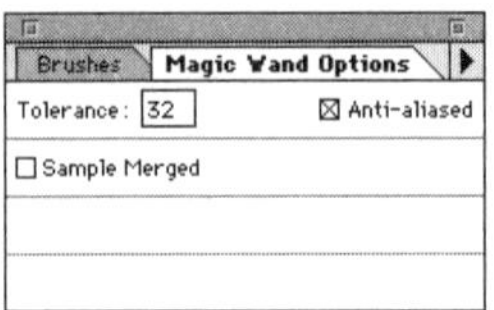

2. Change the Tolerance value to change the size of the colored area selected with the magic wand. The value tells Photoshop how similar colors have to be for the wand to select them.

   For example, if the Tolerance is set to 32 (as it is by default), clicking on a medium blue selection of the sky selects other medium shades of blue, but it doesn't select light and dark blues. If you double the value, you double the number of shades of blue that Photoshop selects.

3. To create hard-edged selections, turn off the Anti-aliased check box.

   For example, if you want to select a black border independently of the rest of an image, change the Tolerance to 0, turn off the Anti-aliased check box, and click on the border.

4. Click on the Sample Merged check box to select pixels on the active layer based on the colors of pixels on other layers.

   Suppose that you've created two layers. The Background layer contains blue sky; the front layer contains a flock of birds. If you want to select an area around the birds on the front layer, turn on Sample Merged and click on the sky with the magic wand.

If you have the Tolerance value set to a low value — say, 0 to10 — and you notice that the magic wand seems to be selecting far too many colors, the culprit is probably the Sample Size setting in the Eyedropper Tool Options palette. To solve the problem, choose the Point Sample option from the pop-up menu in that palette.

More stuff to do with the selection tools

The three selection tools win my vote for the most ingeniously designed tools in Photoshop. They may look like simple little critters, but when used properly, they pack a wallop. The following list explains a bunch of different ways to use these tools.

The first three techniques in the list are explored in great detail in Chapter 12, "The Great Pixel Roundup (Yee Ha)," of that popular title *Photoshop 3 For Macs For Dummies*. The others are covered in Chapter 13, "Making Your Selections Presentable."

Selection Technique	*How You Do It*
Draw a square selection	In most programs, you draw a square by Shift-dragging with the rectangle tool. In Photoshop, you drag-Shift — that is, you press the Shift key *after* you start dragging with the rectangular marquee tool, but before you release. In other words, start dragging, press and hold Shift, continue dragging, release the mouse button, and then release Shift.
Draw a circular selection	Drag-Shift with the elliptical marquee tool to draw a perfectly circular selection outline.
Draw a polygonal selection	To create a selection outline with straight-edges — a polygon — Option-click with the lasso tool. Each point at which you Option-click determines a corner of the polygon.
Add to a selection	Shift-drag with the marquee tool or the lasso tool to retain the present selection and add to it. To add to a selection with the magic wand, Shift-click. For example, if you want to select two rectangular portions of an image, drag with the rectangular marquee tool around one portion of an image and then Shift-drag around the other portion.

(continued)

Selection Technique	How You Do It
Subtract from a selection	To deselect a portion of a selection, ⌘-drag with the marquee or lasso or ⌘-click with the magic wand.
Intersect a selection	If you ⌘-Shift-drag with the marquee or lasso — or ⌘-Shift-click with the magic wand — you deselect everything but the intersecting areas of the previous selection and the new selection.
	Suppose that you select an oval portion of a sky-and-mountain image using the elliptical marquee tool. If you want to deselect the mountains and retain only the sky, ⌘-Shift-click in the sky with the magic wand tool.
Move a selection	Drag the selected area using any of the three selection tools to move it. This leaves a hole where the selection used to be. The hole is colored with the background color (usually white).
Duplicate a selection	Option-drag the selected area with any selection tool to duplicate it. This process is called *cloning*.
Move a selection outline	If you ⌘-Option-drag a selection with one of the selection tools, you move the selection outline without moving the portion of the image inside the selection.
Nudge the selection	Press one of the arrow keys to move the selected area one pixel in that direction.
	TIP: Press Shift with an arrow key to move the selection 10 pixels.
Nudge and duplicate	Press Option with an arrow key to clone the selection and nudge it one pixel. Press Shift-Option-arrow key to clone and nudge 10 pixels.
Drag and drop	When two or more images are open, you can drag the selection from one window and drop it into the other.

Selection Technique	*How You Do It*
	During the drag, the cursor changes to a closed fist when Photoshop is ready for the drop. After the drop, Photoshop duplicates the selection so that it exists in both windows.

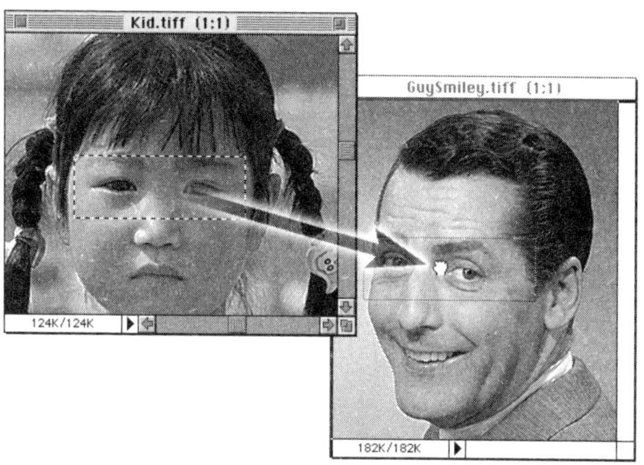

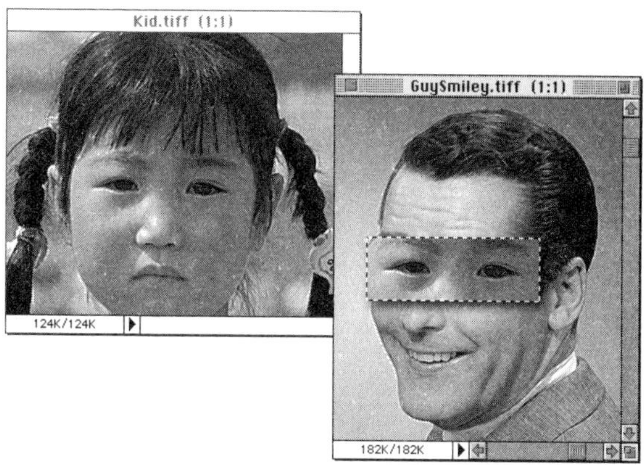

Deselect everything	To deselect the entire image, click anywhere with the marquee or lasso, or click inside the selected area with the magic wand. (You can also choose Select⇨None or press ⌘-D, as described in Part III.)

The Smudge Tool

Drag with the smudge tool to smear pixels around in the image, as if you dragged your finger across a wet oil painting. It's a great way to apply small touch-ups and create finger-painting effects.

Pressing U is a surefire method for selecting the smudge tool.

Changing how the smudge tool works

Most of the options in the Smudge Tool Options palette are familiar from other Options palettes, described earlier in Part I. But a couple are either new or produce special results.

1. Select the smudge tool and press Return to display the Smudge Tool Options palette.

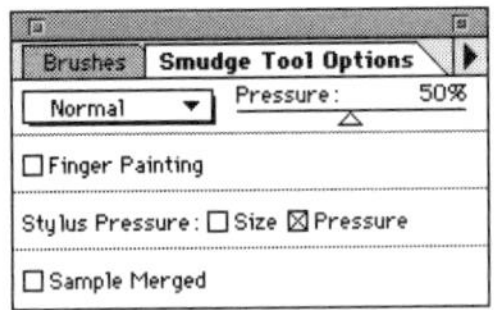

2. Select the Finger Painting check box to smear in a bit of the foreground color at the beginning of the stroke. It's like you dabbed your finger in the foreground color before dragging in the oil painting.

   You can finger paint when the check box is off by Option-dragging with the smudge tool. If the Finger Painting check box is on, Option-dragging smears normally, without introducing the foreground color.

3. Adjust the Pressure slider bar setting to control how far colors smear. When the setting is 50 percent — as it is by default — the colors smear a few pixels. If you set the value to more than 90 percent, the colors smear so far it looks like you're painting.

   As always, you can change the Pressure setting from the keyboard by pressing number keys. Press 1 for 10 percent, 2 for 20 percent, and so on, up to 0 for 100 percent.

4. Select the Sample Merged check box to smear colors from other layers into the active layer.
5. The blend modes work just like they do with the eraser, painting, and rubber stamp tools, except that there are fewer of them. Like the focus tools, the smudge tool offers only seven modes, Normal, Darken, Lighten, Hue, Saturation, Color, and Luminosity.

   For example, if you just want to smear the colors around without disrupting any of the detail in an image, select the Color blend mode. See the "Selecting a blend mode" section of "The Fill Tools: Paint Bucket and Gradient" earlier in Part I to see how the other modes work.
6. Use the Stylus Pressure check boxes as described earlier in the "Working with a pressure-sensitive tablet" section of "The Eraser Tool."

The Toning Tools: Dodge, Burn, and Sponge

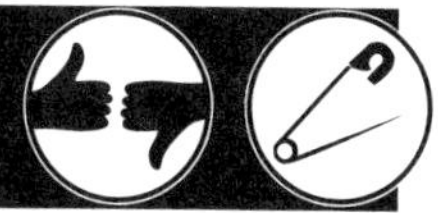

The bottom right tool slot in the toolbox holds three toning tools, which you use to adjust colors in an image.

Toning Tool	How You Use It
Dodge	Drag with this tool to lighten the pixels in the image. For example, you might create highlights with the dodge tool.
	KEY SHORTCUT: Press the O key to select the dodge tool.
Burn	Dragging with the burn tool darkens pixels in the image, which is exactly opposite to the dodge tool. Use this tool to create shadows.
	KEY SHORTCUT: If the dodge tool is selected, press O again to select the burn tool.

(continued)

Toning Tool	How You Use It
	You can also Option-drag with either the dodge or burn tool to produce the effect of the other. Option-dragging with the dodge tool, for example, darkens.
Sponge	Dragging with this tool decreases the saturation of the colors in an image, making them more gray.

When the burn tool is selected, pressing O yet again selects the sponge tool. Keep pressing O to cycle from one toning tool to the next.

Changing how the dodge and burn tools work

You can specify the degree of lightening or darkening that takes place with the dodge and burn tools by changing the settings in the Toning Tools Options palette.

1. Select the dodge or burn tool and press Return to display the Toning Tools Options palette.

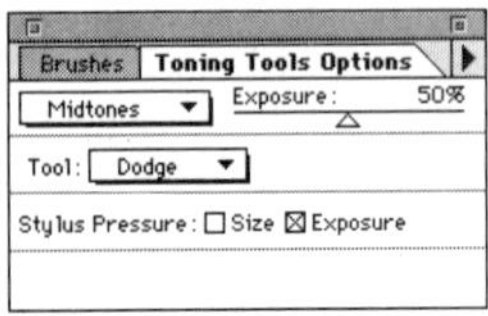

2. Select an option from the pop-up menu in the upper left corner of the palette to change which colors in the image are affected by the toning tool.
    - Select Shadows to lighten or darken only the darkest colors in the image.
    - Choose Midtones to affect only the medium colors.
    - Select Highlights to lighten or darken the lightest colors.

3. Change the Exposure slider bar setting to change how dramatically the toning tool lightens or darkens the image. Higher values produce more noticeable effects.
4. You can select the kind of toning tool from the Tool pop-up menu. But it's a waste of time when you can just press O instead.
5. If you own a pressure-sensitive tablet, change the Stylus Pressure settings to fit your needs, as explained in the "Working with a pressure-sensitive tablet" section of "The Eraser Tool" earlier in Part I.

Note that you can change the settings for the dodge and burn tools completely independently of each other. You might set the dodge tool to lighten Shadows, for example, and set the burn tool to darken Highlights, using different Exposure settings for each.

Changing how the sponge works

When the sponge tool is selected, the Toning Tools Options palette offers different options than it does when the dodge or burn tool is selected.

1. Select the sponge tool and press Return to display the Toning Tools Options palette.

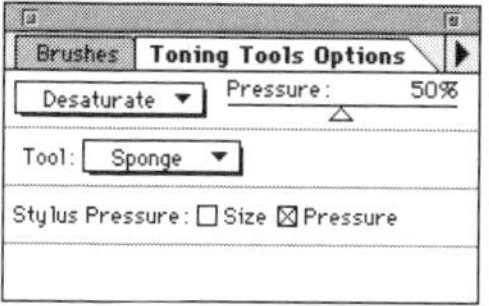

2. Choose the Saturate option from the pop-up menu in the upper left corner of the palette to increase the saturation of colors as you drag over them with the sponge tool.

   Choose Desaturate to make the sponge suck saturation out of colors. This is the default setting of the tool.
3. Change the Pressure slider bar setting to adjust the impact of the sponge tool. Lower settings result in more subtle changes.
4. Ignore the Tool pop-up menu.

5. Turn the Stylus Pressure check boxes on and off to change how Photoshop interprets input from your pressure-sensitive tablet, provided you have one. For more information, see the "Working with a pressure-sensitive tablet" section of "The Eraser Tool" earlier in Part I.

The Type Tool

T

Use the type tool to add type to your image. You cannot edit existing type in the image as you can in a word processor; you can only add new type.

You can select the type tool from the keyboard by pressing Y.

Using the type tool

1. If some portion of the image is selected, choose Select⇨None (or press⌘-D) to deselect it.
2. Select the foreground color in which you want the type to appear. (I explain ways to change the foreground color in "The Eyedropper Tool" and "The Color Controls" earlier in Part I).
3. Select the type tool.
4. Click at the point in the image where you want to add your text. After a few moments, Photoshop displays the Type Tool dialog box.

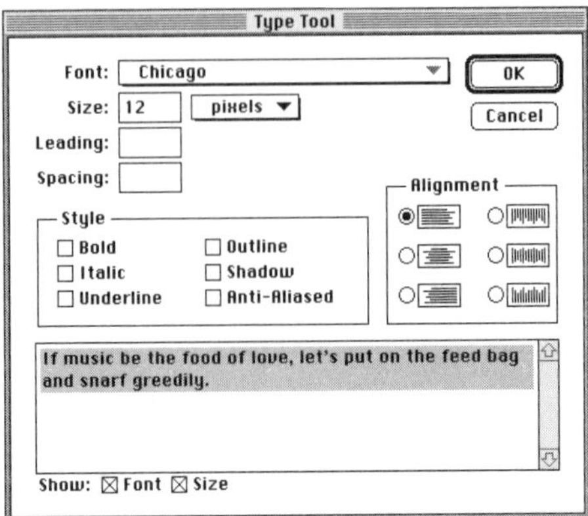

5. Enter the text you want to add. The letters appear in the bottom portion of the dialog box.

Though the text may break naturally from one line to the next inside the dialog box, it will all appear on one line when you add it to the image. If you want more than one line of type, you must insert carriage returns by pressing the Return key.

6. Choose a typeface from the Font pop-up menu. This menu lists every font loaded into your system.

To advance from one option box to the next, press Tab. Press Shift-Tab to go backward. This shortcut works in other Photoshop dialog boxes as well.

7. Enter a type size into the Size option box. Because Photoshop is a pixel-based image editor, larger sizes look better.

8. Enter the amount of space between lines of type into the Leading option box. If you enter no value, Photoshop spaces the lines automatically.

The Leading value is measured from the bottom of one line of type to the bottom of the next. Generally speaking, the Leading value should be between 90 and 120 percent of the Size value.

9. To add or subtract space between characters, enter a positive or negative value into the Spacing option box. Entering no value results in normal spacing.

10. Select check boxes in the Style area to apply type styles such as Bold, Italic, and Underline.

    The Anti-aliased check box smoothes out the rough edges around your type. Normally, you'll want to turn this check box on.

Don't select either Outline or Shadow. Each produces very ugly results. And the two together — well, the results are unspeakable, aren't they?

11. Select an alignment icon to determine whether multiple lines of type are aligned left, centered, or aligned right.

    The three right icons align text up and down. You probably won't want to use these.

12. Press Enter to leave the Type Tool dialog box and add the type to the image.

You can also press Return when the Size, Leading, or Spacing option is active, but it's best to get in the habit of using Enter.

13. Drag the type into place.

For a thorough examination of creating type in Photoshop, read Chapter 15, "Digital Graffiti," in *Photoshop 3 For Macs For Dummies*. You'll even learn how to create a few special effects.

More type tool stuff

After you create your text, it floats above the surface of your image, just like a moved selection. In fact, type *is* a selection, filled with the foreground color. This means that you can apply selection tool techniques. For example, you can ⌘-drag around letters with the marquee or lasso tool to make the letters disappear.

To deselect a letter and set it down in the image, ⌘-drag around it with the type tool. This technique is great for changing the amount of space between letters. When you press ⌘, the type tool cursor changes to a lasso; the tool works like a lasso as long as ⌘ is pressed.

Part II

Photoshop's Palettes

Basic Palette Stuff

Palettes are basically dialog boxes that remain on-screen while you edit an image. They may contain options, such as those found in a dialog box, or icons, such as those found in the toolbox. Click on an icon to perform a function.

Each palette provides its own tiny village of unique options, which I discuss throughout Part II, but all palettes share a few things in common:

- Some palettes contain multiple panels. You can switch to a different panel by clicking on the tab. The tab for the visible panel is white; the tabs for any hidden panels are gray.

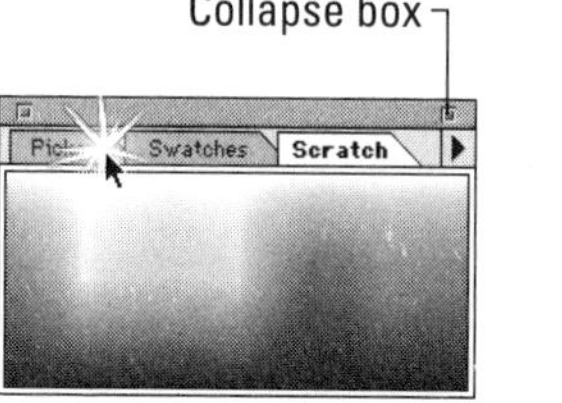

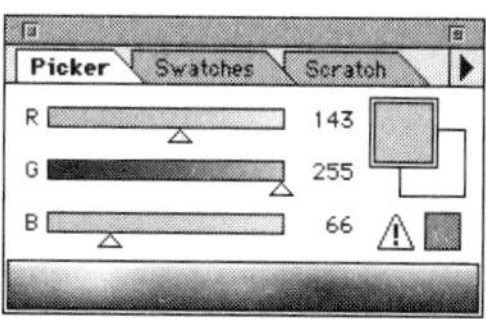

- You can separate a panel off into its own palette by dragging the panel's tab and dropping it outside the palette. You can even drag a panel and drop it into another open palette to combine panels differently.

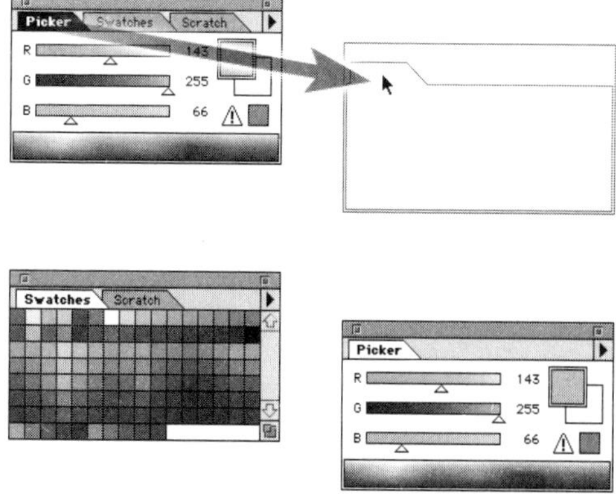

- Click on the collapse box on the right side of the title bar to collapse the palette so only the most essential options at the top of the palette are visible.
- Click on the collapse box again to bring all the options into full view.

- Option-click on the collapse box to hide all but the title bar and the panel tabs. Or double-click on a panel tab.
- Press and hold on the right-pointing arrowhead on the right side of the palette — just below the title bar — to display the palette menu. Different palettes contain different commands.
- You hide and display all panels by choosing commands under the Window⇨Palettes submenu.

The Brushes Palette

The Brushes palette lets you select and edit the brush sizes that affect the bottom eight tools in the toolbox — the eraser, focus, painting, rubber stamp, smudge, and toning tools. When you drag with one of these tools, you create a stroke as thick and as hard or soft as the brush selected in the Brushes palette.

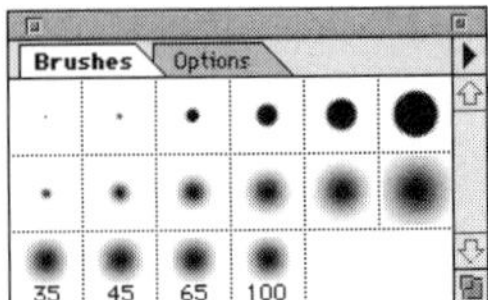

To display the Brushes palette, choose Window⇨Palettes⇨Show Brushes. Choose Window⇨Palettes⇨Hide Brushes to close the palette.

You can also press the F5 key to display and hide the Brushes palette (assuming that you haven't changed any of the function keys, as described in "The Commands Palette" later in Part II).

Setting the brush size

By default, the Brushes palette offers 16 brushes. The first row in the palette contains soft brushes; the rest of the brushes are feathered (softer still). (All brushes are hard when you use the pencil tool.)

To select a brush size, click on the desired brush option in the palette. The brush applies to the selected tool only. For example, if the paintbrush is selected, changing the brush size affects the paintbrush, but not the airbrush.

Photoshop lets you change the brush size using the bracket keys, [and]. These keys work even when the Brushes palette is hidden.

Brush Size Operation	Keyboard Shortcut
Enlarge the brush size	Press the] key to select the next brush size in the palette. This usually has the effect of making the brush larger, but it depends on the order of the brushes in the palette.
Reduce the brush size	Press the [key to select the previous brush. This usually reduces the size of the brush, depending on the order of brushes in the palette.
Select the first brush	Press Shift-[to select the very first brush size in the Brushes palette. By default, this is the single-pixel brush.
Select the last brush	Press Shift-] to select the very last brush size in the Brushes palette.

Creating your own brush

Photoshop lets you create and modify brush sizes. You can create larger brushes, increase or decrease the feathering, and even rotate the brush to create calligraphic effects.

1. Decide whether you want to modify one of the existing brushes or create your own.
   - To modify a selected brush, choose Brush Options from the palette menu. Or just double-click on the brush you want to change.

- To create a new brush, choose New Brush from the palette menu. Or simply click in an empty spot at the bottom of the palette.

  Either way, a dialog box full of brush-making options appears on-screen.

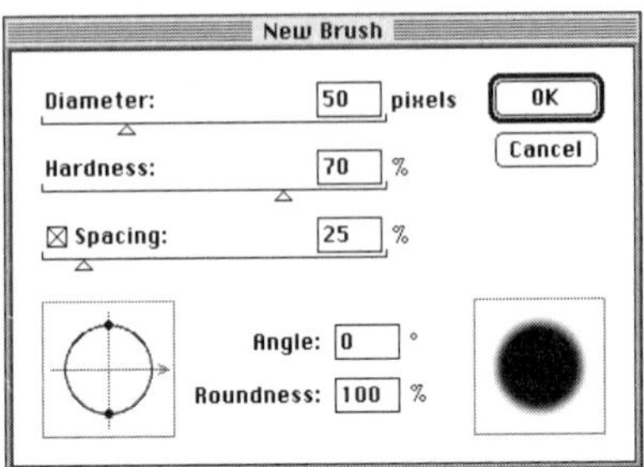

2. Drag the Diameter slider to make the brush bigger or smaller. If you know the exact width value you want to use — in pixels — enter it into the option box on the right side of the slider.
3. Change the Hardness value to make the brush more or less blurry. A value of 100 percent produces crisp but antialiased edges. Anything else is progressively fuzzier. (The 10 feathered brushes in the Brushes palette have Hardness values of 0 percent.)
4. In “The Eraser Tool” in Part I, I explained how painting and editing tools lay down dollops of paint. You can change the space between dollops by altering the Spacing value. The value is measured as a percentage of the diameter of the brush.
5. Turn off the Spacing check box to scatter dollops of paint according to how fast you drag with a tool. You’ll see exactly what I mean by “dollops.”
6. Change the Roundness value to make the brush oval instead of round. A value of 100 percent is absolutely circular; anything less results in a shape that is shorter than it is wide.

You can also drag one of the two handles at the top and bottom of the circle in the lower left corner of the dialog box to squish the brush shape.

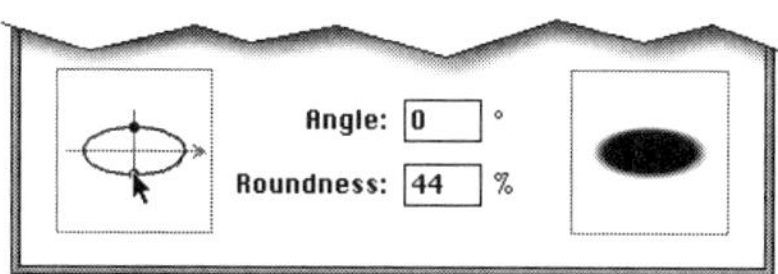

7. Change the Angle value to rotate an oval brush.

   Better yet, drag the little gray arrow to the right of the circle in the lower left corner of the dialog box.

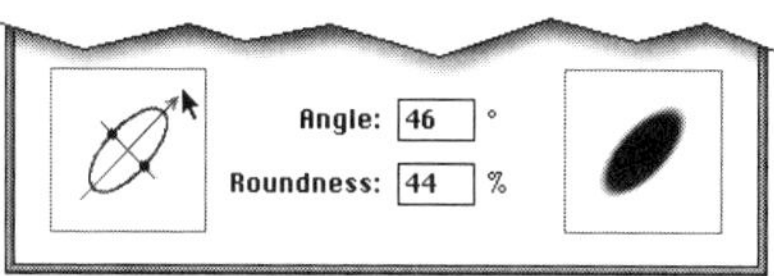

8. Press Return to exit the dialog box and add the modified brush to the Brushes palette.

Other brush stuff

The Brushes palette menu offers some more commands that let you manage your brush collection.

Brushes Palette Command	What It Does
Delete Brush	Choose this command to delete the selected brush size from the Brushes palette. You can also delete a brush by ⌘-clicking on it. (When the cursor is inside the Brushes palette, pressing the ⌘ key changes it to a little pair of scissors to show you what's in store.)
Define Brush	To create a custom brush, select an area in your image and choose the Define Brush command. This adds the selection to the palette so that you can paint with it.

(continued)

Brushes Palette Command	What It Does
	You can edit a custom brush by double-clicking on it. You can change the Spacing value or deselect the Anti-aliased check box to give the brush hard edges. (The latter is dimmed when you edit large brushes.)
Reset Brushes	To return to the 16 default brushes, choose the Reset Brushes command and click on the OK button. (To add the original 16 to the other brushes in the palette, click on the Append button.)
Load Brushes	Photoshop includes three collections of predefined brushes on disk. These brushes are located in the Brushes & Patterns folder inside the Goodies folder (in the same folder that contains the Photoshop application). The Assorted Brushes file, for example, includes 38 custom brushes such as symbols, sparkles, and an eyeball. To open a brush collection and get rid of the other brushes in the palette, choose Load Brushes.

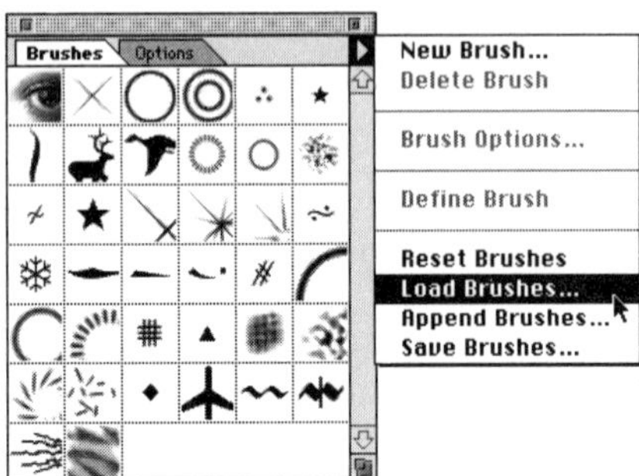

Brushes Palette Command	What It Does
Append Brushes	To add a collection of brushes from disk to the existing brushes in the palette, choose the Append Brushes command.

Brushes Palette Command	What It Does
Save Brushes	This command saves all the brushes in the Brushes palette to disk so that you can use them later.

The Channels Palette

The Channels palette serves two purposes:

- You can examine the independent color channels in a full-color image. For example, you can edit the red channel separately from the green and blue channels in an RGB image.
- You can store selections as masks. This allows you to re-use the selections at a later time.

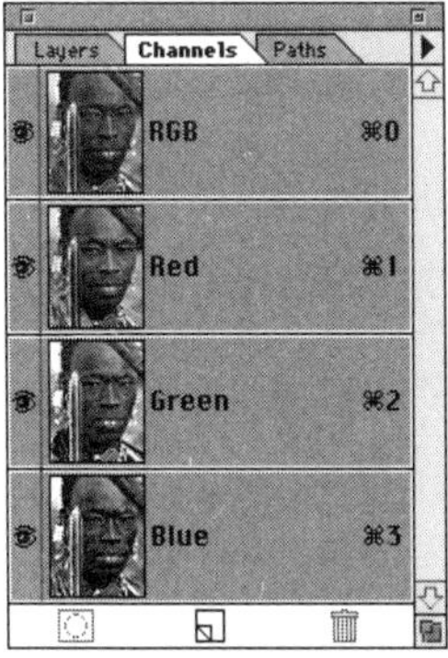

Display the Channels palette by choosing Window➪Palettes➪Show Channels. To hide the palette, choose Window➪Palettes➪Hide Channels. (This is one of the few palettes with no keyboard shortcut.)

Navigating channels

The first item in the Channels palette represents the composite view of the image — that is, the view that shows all colors at once. The next few items show each independent color channel on its own.

- In an RGB image, you see three independent color channels — Red, Green, and Blue.
- A Lab image contains three independent channels as well — one for luminosity and two channels labeled arbitrarily *a* and *b*.
- A CMYK image contains four independent color channels — Cyan, Magenta, Yellow, and Black.
- Grayscale images, black-and-white bitmaps, and indexed images with only 256 colors contain only one image channel.

Any items beyond the basic color channels are considered mask channels (also known in some circles as *alpha channels*, so named because they are channels without specific purposes).

For a complete picture of using and navigating color channels, read Chapter 6, "Auntie Em versus the Munchkins (Death Match)," in *Photoshop 3 For Macs For Dummies*.

But on the off chance that you have no intention of buying that book — oh, come on, it's really good, everyone says so — the following list tells you how to get around:

Channel Navigation	***How You Do It***
Switch channels	Click on a channel in the Channels palette. The channel on which you click becomes tinted with gray. Any edits applied to the image window affect the active channel only.
	Press ⌘ plus a number to switch channels from the keyboard. For example, in an RGB image, ⌘-1 takes you to the red channel and ⌘-0 takes you back to the full-color composite view.
Edit multiple channels	To edit more than one channel at a time, click on one channel and then Shift-click on the other. For example, if you want to edit both the red and blue channels, click on the Red item in the palette and then Shift-click on Blue.

Channel Navigation	How You Do It
Display an inactive channel	Just because you want to edit a single channel doesn't mean that you can't view all of them. Just click in the left column next to an inactive channel to display it. An eyeball icon appears to show that the channel is visible.
Hide a channel	To hide a channel, click on its eyeball icon.
Scale the thumbnails	By default, the Channels palette includes dinky little thumbnails showing the contents of each channel. You can make these previews larger by choosing Palette Options from the palette menu. Select a different radio button and press Return.

Masking stuff

All channels other than the necessary color channels qualify as mask channels. But you can use the color channels as masks — or at least, the starting point for masks — as well.

A mask channel works very much like the quick mask mode, as explained in Part I. You can view mask and image together, in which case the mask looks like a color overlay. Or you can view the mask by itself, in which case the deselected areas appear black and the selected areas appear white.

Masking Operation	How You Do It
Save a selection as a mask	To convert the selection to a mask, click on the convert selection icon, which is that little dotted circle in the lower left corner of the Channels palette. Photoshop adds another channel to the palette.

(continued)

Masking Operation	How You Do It
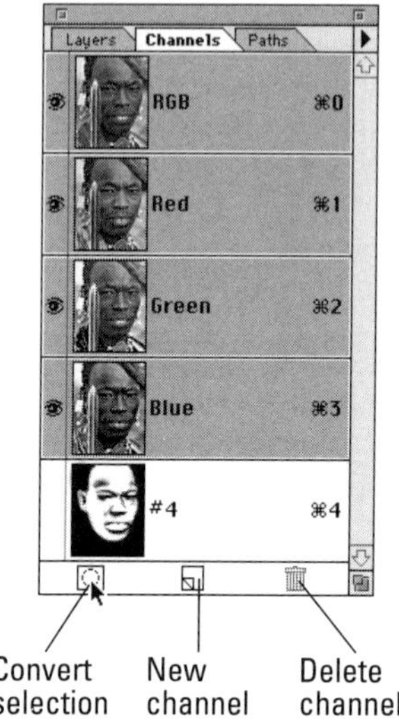	
Duplicate a channel	To duplicate a channel, choose the Duplicate Channel command from the palette menu. This allows you to create a mask based on an existing channel in the image.
TIP	You can also duplicate a channel by dragging it onto the new channel icon — that little folded page at the bottom of the palette.
Create a blank mask	If you want to create the mask from scratch, click on the new channel icon (or choose New Channel from the palette menu).
	A dialog box appears, asking you to name the channel and confirm its overlay color. After you press Return, a completely black channel appears at the bottom of the palette.
	To bypass the dialog box, Option-click on the new channel icon.

Masking Operation	*How You Do It*
View the image	To see the mask and image together — as in the quick mask mode — click in the left-hand column next to the composite view to toggle the eyeball icon. Click again to hide the image.
Change the color overlay	Choose Channel Options or just double-click on the mask channel to display a dialog box that lets you name the channel and change the color overlay. See "Quick Mask Icons" in Part I for an explanation of the specific options.
Convert to a selection	To convert any channel to a selection outline, Option-click on the mask channel in the palette.
	KEY SHORTCUT: Press ⌘ and Option plus a number key to convert the channel to a selection. For example, ⌘-Option-4 makes a selection outline from the fourth channel in the palette.
	TIP: You can also Shift-Option-click on a channel to add it to the existing selection. Or ⌘-Option-click on the channel to subtract it from the selection. Or ⌘-Shift-Option-click to find the intersection.
Delete a channel	To delete a mask channel from the palette, choose the Delete Channel command from the palette menu. Or better yet, drag the channel onto the trash icon in the lower right corner of the palette.
	REMEMBER: You can delete mask channels only. You cannot delete color channels because they are necessary to the image.

More channel stuff

The Channels palette includes three commands that you're unlikely to ever use. They represent specialized niche functions that about one in 100 users will find helpful, and even that is probably an exaggeration. But just in case, here's a look:

Channels Palette Command	What It Does
Video Alpha	If you own a 32-bit video-editing board, such as the TrueVision NuVista+, Photoshop lets you copy a mask channel to the board's alpha channel. You can then overlay a Photoshop image onto live video (a technique called *chroma keying*). Very few video boards offer this option. Check the documentation that came with the board for the term *chroma key*. If you can't find the term, ignore the Video Alpha command.
Split Channels	This command splits off every channel in your image into its own image window. You might use the command to split off masks into independent files. Then you can reassemble the color channels using the Merge Channels command.
Merge Channels	After splitting channels, you can put them back together by choosing this command. A dialog box appears, asking you what kind of image you want to create — RGB, CMYK, Lab, or Multichannel (which is a loose collection of channels discussed in "Mode⇨Multichannel" in Part III). Then you select which image should go with each channel.

The Color Palette: Picker, Swatches, and Scratch

Photoshop provides three color panels all clustered together inside a single palette.

Color Panel	*How It Works*
Picker	This panel lets you change the foreground or background color by dragging slider bars. It's the most useful of the three color panels.
Swatches	The Swatches panel lets you assemble a collection of colors that you intend to use over and over when painting in Photoshop.
Scratch	This panel is simply an additional little image window that you can use to create patterns and custom brushes or blend colors to create new colors.

You can display the palette by choosing Window➪Palette➪Show Picker, Window➪Palette➪Show Swatches, or Window➪Palette➪Show Scratch, depending on which panel you want to use.

You can also press the F6 key to display or hide the palette (assuming that you haven't changed the function keys as I describe later in "The Commands Palette"). The Picker panel appears in front.

Using the Picker panel

If the Color Picker dialog box is a little bit too jam-packed for your tastes — goodness knows it is for mine — you can edit the foreground and background color more expediently in the Picker palette.

1. Press F6 to display the Picker panel.

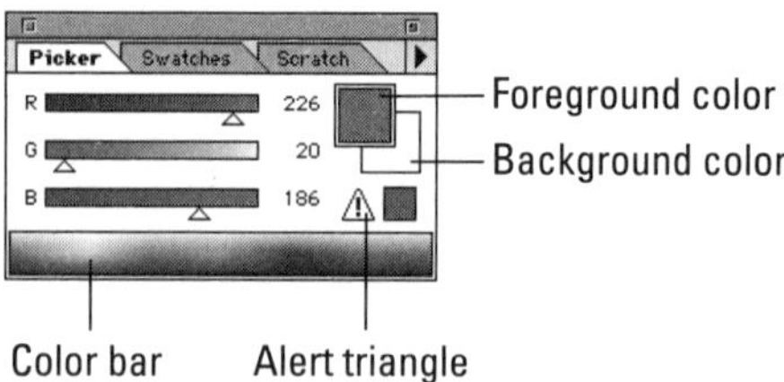

2. Click on the foreground or background square on the right side of the palette to decide which color you want to change.

Selecting the background color icon reverses the performance of the eyedropper tool as long as the Picker palette is visible. When the background color icon is selected, clicking with the eyedropper changes the background color and Option-clicking changes the foreground color.

3. Choose the color model you want to use — grayscale, RGB, HSB, CMYK, or Lab — from the palette menu. (For information on how these work, see "The Color Controls" in Part I.)

4. Drag the slider bar triangles to edit the color. The values to the right of the sliders update to show you the amount of primary color added.

   - The grayscale and CMYK values range from 0 percent (the lightest) to 100 percent (the darkest).
   - The RGB values range from 0 (the darkest) to 255 (the lightest).
   - The H in HSB is measured in 360 degrees on an imaginary color wheel. S and B are measured from 0 to 100 percent.
   - In Lab, the L value varies from 0 (the darkest) to 100 (the lightest). The abstract *a* and *b* values range from –120 to 120.

   The good news is that Photoshop colors the sliders to show you what effect they have on your color. For example, if the right tip of the G slider is yellow, dragging the triangle in that direction changes the color to yellow.

You can even click right on the color in the slider bar that you want to select. To change the color to yellow in the previous example, you can just click on the portion of the G slider bar that appears yellow.

You can access the color slider bars only when working on color images. When you're editing a grayscale image, Photoshop displays the K (or black) slider only.

5. If Photoshop can't print the color, it displays an alert triangle in the lower right corner of the palette. The color square next to the triangle shows the nearest printable color. Click on the triangle or color square to select the printable color.

If you can't quite get the knack of the slider bars, you can use the color bar at the bottom of the palette instead. The color bar devotes a single pixel to each of roughly 4,000 colors available in Photoshop. Just click on a pixel in the color bar to select its color.

Option-click in the color bar to change the background color when the foreground color icon is active or to change the foreground color when the background color icon is active.

By default, the color bar shows CMYK colors, so every one of them is printable. If you want to change the color bar, choose the Color Bar command from the palette menu. After the dialog box appears, select an option from the Style pop-up menu.

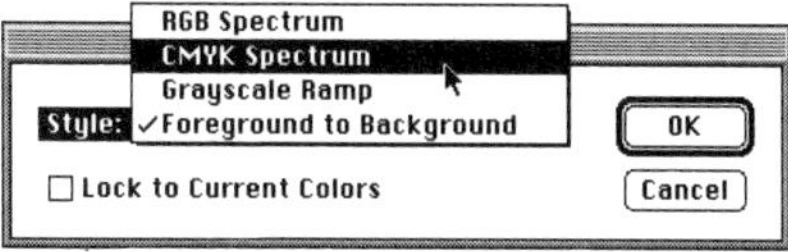

You can alternatively display the Color Bar dialog box by ⌘-clicking on the color bar at the bottom of the Picker palette.

The most interesting option in the Style pop-up menu is Foreground to Background, which fills the color bar with a gradation of colors between the foreground and background colors. The color bar updates as you change the foreground and background colors. If you don't want the color bar to update, select the Lock to Current Colors check box.

Using the Swatches panel

Use the Swatches panel to store frequently used colors, making them easier to access.

1. Press F6 and then click on the Swatches tab to display the Swatches panel.

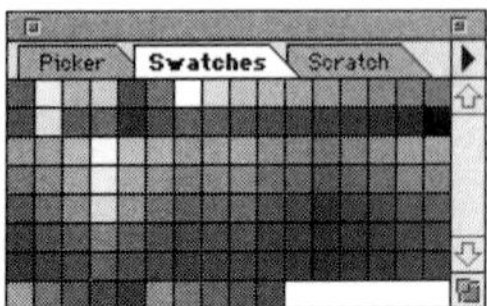

2. Click on a color in the palette to make it the foreground color.
3. Option-click on a color to make it the background color.
4. To add the foreground color to the palette, move the cursor over a blank area where there are no swatches. The cursor changes to a paint bucket. Then click. Photoshop adds a new swatch.

   To replace a swatch with the foreground color, Shift-click on it. To insert a new swatch before an existing swatch, Shift-Option-click on it.

5. To delete a color swatch, ⌘-click on it. The cursor changes to a pair of scissors when you ⌘-click.
6. To save the current collection of swatches to disk, choose the Save Swatches command from the palette menu.
7. To load a collection of swatches saved to disk, choose the Load Swatches command from the palette menu. Photoshop offers many predefined collections from Pantone, Trumatch, and other vendors in the Color Palettes folder inside the Goodies folder (in the same folder that contains Photoshop).

   If you don't want Photoshop to replace the color swatches presently in the palette, choose the Append Swatches command instead.

8. To restore the default 122 colors in the palette, choose Reset Swatches from the palette menu.

Using the Scratch panel

You can use the Scratch panel like a little doodling pad, trying out color combinations, brush sizes, and so forth.

1. Press F6 and then click on the Scratch tab to display the Scratch panel.

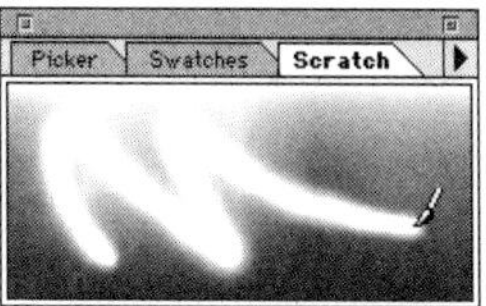

2. Abuse the scratch pad — the central portion of the Scratch palette — to your heart's content. You can use any painting or editing tool. You can even select an area inside the scratch pad.
3. To paste something into the pad, choose the Paste command from the palette menu. You can also copy the selected area by choosing the Copy command from the palette menu.
4. To fill a selected area inside the pad with the background color, choose the Clear command from the palette menu.
5. To select a color from the scratch pad, click on it using the eyedropper tool.

   If you choose the Locked command from the palette menu, Photoshop doesn't let you modify the contents of the scratch pad. All you can do is select colors from it. Whether the eyedropper is selected or not, clicking on a locked pad changes the foreground color; Option-clicking changes the background color.

   To unlock the pad, choose the Locked command again.
6. You can save the contents of the scratch pad to disk by choosing the Save Scratch command from the palette menu.
7. To load a saved scratch pad, choose the Load Scratch command.
8. To restore the original scratch pad, choose Reset Scratch from the palette menu.

The Commands Palette

The Commands palette lets you assign your own keyboard equivalents to commands inside Photoshop. The palette is not without problems, but it's the only way to make frequently used commands such as Image⇨Canvas Size and Select⇨Color Range available from the keyboard.

Commands	
Undo	F1
Cut	F2
Copy	F3
Paste	F4
Show Brushes	F5
Show Picker	F6
Hide Layers	F7
Hide Info	F8
Hide Commands	F9
Fill	↑F5
Feather	↑F6
Inverse	↑F7

Choose Window⇨Palettes⇨Show Commands to display the Commands palette. Or press F9. (You can change this and other function key shortcuts inside the Commands palette.)

Each item in the Commands palette lists a command and its shortcut key. Each item is also a button. So to access the command, you can either press the key listed on the button or simply click directly on the button.

Adding new keyboard shortcuts

You can assign any function key — F1 through F15 — to a command. You can also assign combinations of Shift and function keys. This makes for 30 possible keyboard shortcuts. Of these, only 12 are taken by default, leaving another 18 free for you to assign as you see fit.

If you prefer to click on the buttons in the Commands palette, you can assign as many commands to buttons as you like. Whether you want to assign a function-key shortcut to a command or simply create a button, follow these steps:

1. Press F9 to display the Commands palette.
2. Choose New Command from the palette menu. The New Command dialog box appears.

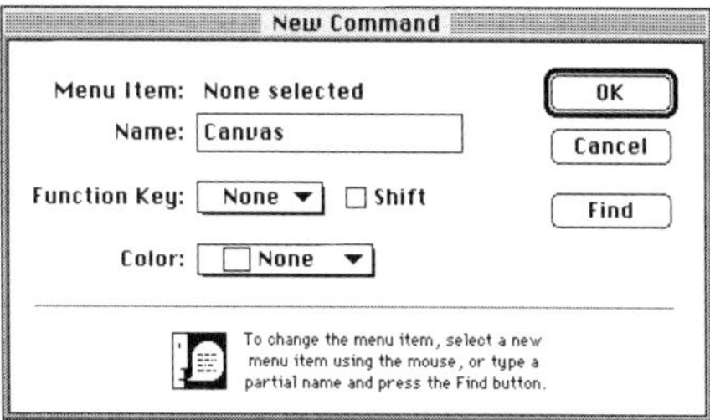

3. You can select the command to which you want to assign a shortcut or button in two ways:
   - Choose the command from the menu.
   - Enter the first few letters of the command into the Name option box. Don't enter the menu name, just the command name. For Image⇨Canvas Size, for example, enter the word *Canvas.* Then click on the Find button. Photoshop locates the matching command.

   If you don't care about keyboard shortcuts and only want to create a button for a command, skip Steps 4 and 5.

4. Do you want to assign just a function key or Shift plus a function key? If you want to do the latter, select the Shift check box.
5. Assign a function key by choosing one from the Function Key pop-up menu. The pop-up menu lists only those keys that are not yet assigned.
6. You can assign one of eight colors to the button in the Commands palette by choosing an option from the Colors pop-up menu.
7. Press Return to exit the dialog box and add a new button to the Commands palette.

Changing keyboard shortcuts

Five of the 12 default function-key shortcuts are assigned to commands that already have shortcuts.

Command	Existing Shortcut	Redundant Function Key
Edit⇨Undo	⌘-Z	F1
Edit⇨Cut	⌘-X	F2
Edit⇨Copy	⌘-C	F3
Edit⇨Paste	⌘-V	F4
Edit⇨Fill	Shift-Delete	Shift-F5

Personally, I prefer to reassign F1, F2, F3, F4, and Shift-F5 to commands that have no shortcuts. You might also want to reassign other function keys, apply different colors to the buttons, or move the button up or down in the palette. Here's how:

1. Choose Edit Commands from the Commands palette menu to display the Edit Commands dialog box. All buttons appear in a scrolling list.

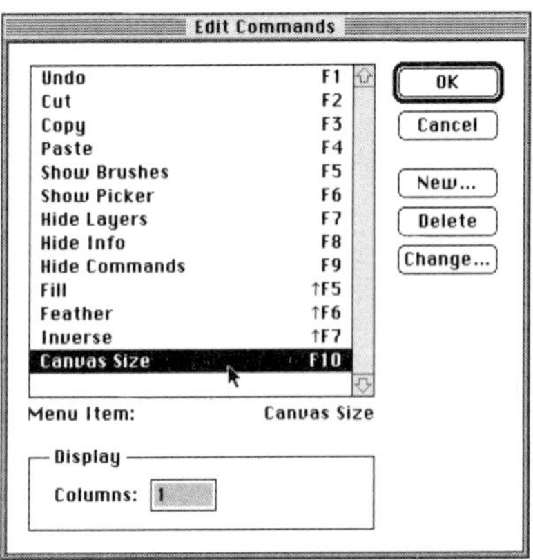

2. To change one of the commands, select the command name in the scrolling list and then click on the Change button. Or just double-click on the command name.

   Either way, the Change Command dialog box appears, which is identical in all respects to the New Command dialog box described in the preceding steps.

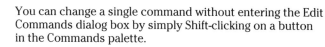

You can change a single command without entering the Edit Commands dialog box by simply Shift-clicking on a button in the Commands palette.

3. To delete a command in the Edit Commands dialog box, select the command name and click on the Delete button.

You can also delete a command name by ⌘-clicking on it. This technique even works outside the Edit Commands dialog box. Just ⌘-click on a button to delete it.

4. To add a new command, click on the New button. Photoshop displays the New Command dialog box, described in the previous steps.
5. You can move a command by dragging it up or down in the list.
6. Enter a different value into the Columns option box to arrange the buttons in the Commands palette into multiple columns. This feature is especially useful if the buttons won't fit on-screen when arranged in a single column.
7. Press the Return key to exit the dialog box and make the changes.

Other command stuff

Like the Brushes and Swatches palettes described earlier, the Commands palette allows you to save commands to disk so that you can load them again later.

Commands Palette Command	*What It Does*
Reset Commands	To restore the 12 default buttons to the Commands palette, choose Reset Commands from the palette menu.
Load Commands	Photoshop ships with five sets of predefined commands on disk. These are located in the Command Sets folder inside the Goodies folder (in the same folder that contains the Photoshop application). To open a set of commands and replace the other buttons in the palette, choose Load Commands.

(continued)

Commands Palette Command	*What It Does*
Append Commands	To add a command set to the existing buttons in the palette, choose Append Commands instead.
Save Commands	Choose this command to save your modified command buttons to disk for later use.

Photoshop may occasionally revert to the default palette buttons (if the preference settings become corrupted, for example). But as long as you saved your commands to disk, you can always reinstate them by choosing Load Commands.

The Info Palette

The Info palette provides numerical feedback as you perform certain operations. This feedback is especially helpful when you're gauging CMYK colors for four-color printing and scaling or rotating a selection.

For example, when you rotate a selection (after choosing Image⇨Rotate⇨Free), the Info palette lists the precise angle of rotation as it occurs.

You can display the Info palette by choosing Window⇨Palettes⇨Show Info. Or press F8 to either hide or show the palette.

Reading the Info palette

Instead of word labels, Photoshop uses icons to identify the items in the Info palette. Here's what each of the icons means:

Info Palette Icon	*What It Means*
 Color readouts	Photoshop provides two sets of color readouts, one in the current color model — grayscale, RGB, and so forth — and one in CMYK. These color readouts explain the color of the exact pixel underneath the cursor. When you're working in the CMYK mode, the Info palette lists just one set of color readouts (unless you change the preference settings, as described shortly).  If a color cannot be printed, exclamation points follow the CMYK values. The CMYK values represent the closest printable colors. When you're working inside a color correction dialog box — such as Levels or Curves (both discussed in Part III) — the Info palette lists two values for each primary color, separated by a slash. The value before the slash is the color of the pixel before the color correction; the value after the slash is the color after the correction.
Mouse coordinates	The Info palette always lists the horizontal and vertical coordinates of the cursor, measured from the upper left corner of the image window.
Anchor point	When you drag with the crop tool or one of the marquee tools, the anchor icon indicates the point at which you began dragging. As soon as you stop dragging, this icon disappears.

(continued)

Info Palette Icon	*What It Means*
Width and height	These values tell the maximum width and height of the selected area inside the image. These are among the only values that remain visible even when the cursor is not positioned inside an image window.
Perpendicular distances	When you drag with the line or gradient tool, the Info palette lists the horizontal and vertical distances of the drag. As soon as you stop dragging, this icon disappears.
Angle (and distance)	When you drag with the line or gradient tool, the Info palette also lists the angle of the drag (in degrees) and the direct distance. Again, the icon disappears after you stop dragging. When you rotate a selection (using Image⇨Rotate⇨Free), this icon tells the angle of rotation in degrees. When you are cropping an image, it tells the angle of the crop marquee. The icon remains visible as long as the rotation or crop is in progress.
Scale	When you scale a selection using Image⇨Effects⇨Scale, this icon tells the horizontal and vertical extent of the scaling, measured as percentages. These values remain visible as long as the scaling is in progress.

Changing the Info palette readouts

You can change how the Info palette lists color readouts and mouse coordinates by choosing the Palette Options command from the Info palette menu.

1. Press F8 to display the Info palette.
2. Choose Palette Options from the palette menu. The Info Options dialog box appears.

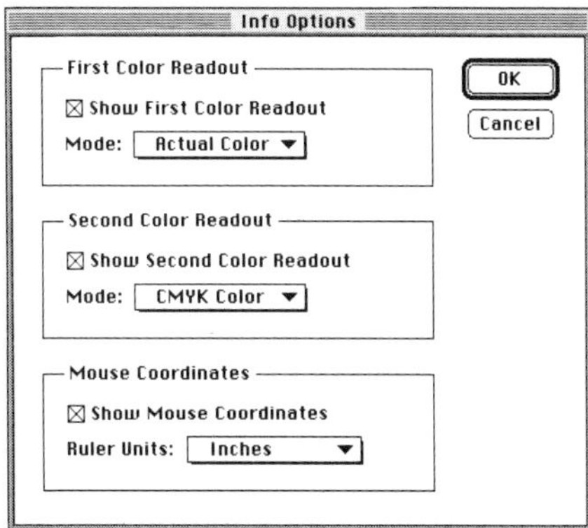

3. To specify whether the first set of color readouts appears in the palette, turn the Show First Color Readout check box on or off.

4. Select an option from the Mode pop-up menu to determine how the Info palette describes the color of the pixel under the cursor:

   - The Actual Color option describes the color in the image's active color mode. For example, when you're editing an RGB image, the Info palette lists the RGB values. When you're editing in grayscale, it lists a single K (black) value.
   - Select the Grayscale option to display a single K value regardless of the active color mode. The value is measured from 0 (white) to 100 percent (black).
   - The RGB Color option lists red, green, and blue values regardless of the active color mode. These values are measured from 0 (no color, dark) to 255 (full color, light).
   - The HSB Color option lists hue, saturation, and brightness values regardless of the active color mode. The H value is measured in degrees; the other two are measured as percentages.
   - The CMYK Color option lists cyan, magenta, yellow, and black values regardless of the active color mode. The values are measured from 0 (no color, light) to 100 percent (full color, dark).

- Lab lists luminosity and *a* and *b* values regardless of the active color mode. Luminosity is measured from 0 to 100 percent; *a* and *b* are measured from –120 to 120.
- The final option, Total Ink, lists the total amount of cyan, magenta, yellow, and black ink that must be printed to represent a color. This option is strictly for pre-press operators and other technical types.

5. Modify the Second Color Readout options in the same ways described in Steps 3 and 4.
6. Turn the Show Mouse Coordinates check box on or off to tell Photoshop whether or not to display the mouse coordinate icon in the Info palette.
7. Select a system of measurement from the Ruler Units pop-up menu to control the units used to measure all distances in Photoshop. This option controls the units used for the mouse coordinates, anchor point, width and height, and distance values in the Info palette.

   It also controls the units used in the rulers (displayed by choosing Window⇨Show Rulers) as well as the New Image, Image Size, and Canvas Size dialog boxes and the Cropping Tool Options palette. You can select from Pixels (my favorite), Inches (the default setting), Centimeters (metric), Points ($^1/_{72}$ inches), or Picas ($^1/_6$ inches). You can also change the unit of measure by choosing File⇨Preferences⇨ Units, as described in Part III, but using the Info palette is more convenient.
8. Press the Return key to exit the dialog box and accept any changes.

You can access the pop-up menu options without entering the Info Options dialog box. Just click and hold on one of the color readout or mouse coordinate icons to display a pop-up menu of options.

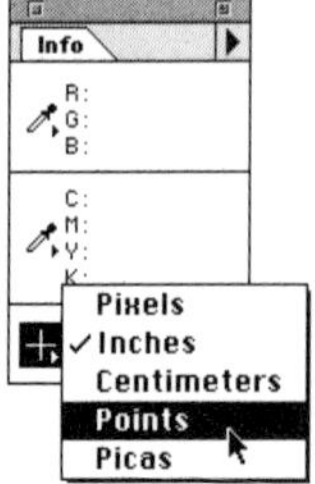

The Layers Palette

Photoshop lets you mix images together by creating layers. Each layer remains independent of the others, even though the image as a whole may appear to blend together seamlessly.

The Layers palette lets you create and modify independent layers in an image. You can also apply special masks to layers and merge layers back together from the Layers palette.

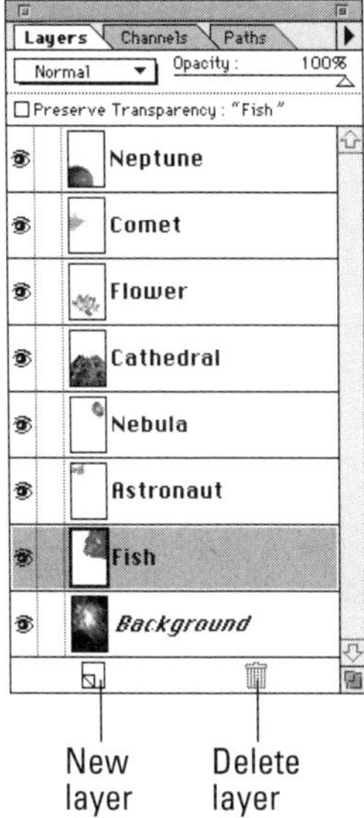

Display the Layers palette by choosing Window⇨Palettes⇨Show Layers. Or press F7 to hide or display the palette.

For the complete picture on using layers in Photoshop, read Chapter 18, "I Sing the Image Amalgam," in *Photoshop 3 For Macs For Dummies.*

Creating a layer

Every image you open in Photoshop contains one layer, which is labeled *Background* in the Layers palette. This Background layer is completely opaque and represents the rearmost layer in the image. Any layers added to the image will appear in front of this layer.

The following steps explain how to take a portion of an image and send it to its own layer.

1. Select part of an image using any selection tool.
2. Choose Select⇨Float, which clones the selection and makes it hover in front of the rest of the image. Photoshop adds a new item called *Floating Selection* to the Layers palette.

   The selection is now independent of the image, but its independence is only temporary. If you deselect the floating selection, it falls back into place. (For more information on floating, see "Select⇨Float" in Part III.)
3. Choose the Make Layer command from the Layers palette menu. A dialog box appears, asking you to name the layer.

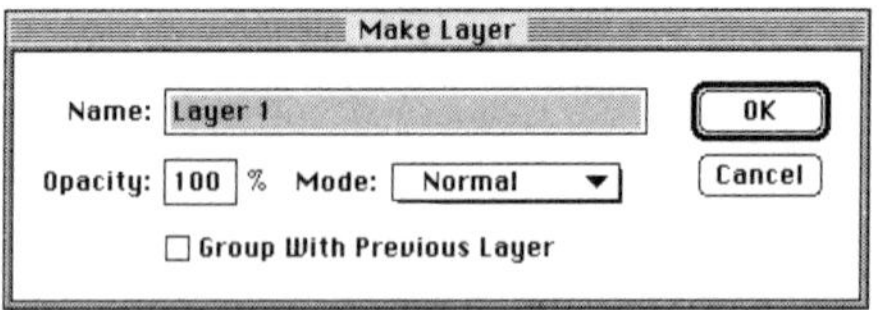

   - Instead of choosing the command, you can simply click on the new layer icon, which is the folded page in the bottom left corner of the palette. Or double-click on the Floating Selection item.
   - To bypass the Make Selection dialog box and have Photoshop name the layer automatically, Option-click on the new layer icon or Option-double-click on the Floating Selection item in the Layers palette. This way, you can skip Steps 4 and 5.
4. Enter a name for the layer into the Name option box.

   You can change the other options — Opacity, Mode, and Group With Previous Layer — more conveniently from other locations. So for now, ignore them.

5. Press Return to exit the dialog box and create the new layer. The new layer name appears in the Layers palette.

Notice that the selection outline disappears. The selection is no longer needed because the layer is completely independent of the rest of the image.

Here are a few additional ways to add layers to an image in Photoshop:

Layer Operation	*How You Do It*
Create a blank layer	You can paint inside an image without doing any permanent damage by first creating a new, transparent layer. To do this, make sure that the selected area — if there is one — is not floating. Then click on the new layer icon in the Layers palette or choose the New Layer command from the palette menu.  To bypass the New Layer dialog box, Option-click on the new layer icon.
Duplicate a layer	You can make an exact copy of the active layer by choosing the Duplicate Layer command from the Layers palette menu. Or better yet, drag the layer onto the new layer icon at the bottom of the palette.
Drag and drop selection	If you drag and drop a selection from a different image window (as described in "The Selection Tools: Marquee, Lasso, and Magic Wand" in Part I), Photoshop imports the selection as a floating selection. Option-click on the new layer icon to convert the floating selection into a layer.
Drag and drop image	If you drag and drop a deselected image or layer from one window to another using the move tool (as described in "The Move Tool" in Part I), Photoshop automatically assigns the dropped image to its own layer.

Navigating layers

After you establish one or more layers in an image, you can move between layers and modify layers as follows:

Layer Navigation	*How You Do It*
Switch layers	You can activate a layer by clicking on its name in the Layers palette. The layer becomes tinted with gray to show that it's active. Any edits applied to the image window affect the active layer only.
	TIP: Press ⌘-] to activate the next layer up. Press ⌘-[to activate the next layer down. Press ⌘-Option-] to activate the top layer; press ⌘-Option-[to activate the bottom layer.
	Using the move tool, you can ⌘-click on a detail in the image window to activate the layer on which the detail resides.
	REMEMBER: Switching layers doesn't affect the selection outline. This means that you can select part of Layer 1, switch to Layer 2, and then use the selection outline to modify the image on Layer 2.
Hide a layer	To hide a layer, click on the eyeball icon to the left of the layer name.
Hide all but one layer	TIP: To hide all layers but one, Option-click on the eyeball icon in front of the layer you want to remain visible.
Show layers	Click in the eyeball column in front of a hidden layer to make the layer visible. If only one layer is visible, Option-click on the eyeball icon to the left of that layer name to make all layers visible.
Move an entire layer	To move the active layer, drag it with the move tool. As long as no portion of the layer is selected, the entire layer moves.

Layer Navigation	How You Do It
Move multiple layers	Though there's no way to edit multiple layers at a time, you can move multiple layers with the move tool. Click in the second column — just to the right of the eyeball — next to a layer that is *not* active. A move icon (like the move tool) appears in front of both the active layer name and the name of the layer you clicked. Now drag with the move tool to move both layers at once.

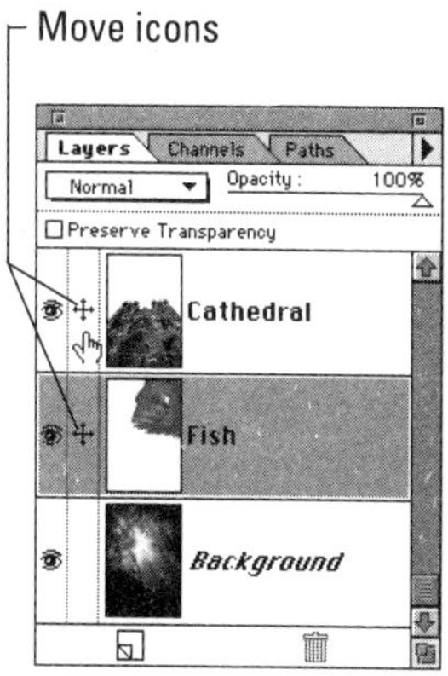

Move icons

Layer Navigation	How You Do It
Move forward or backward	Drag a layer up or down in the Layers palette to move it in front or in back of other layers. A horizontal black bar shows where the layer will fall when you release. You can even move the Floating Selection item forward and backward. But you cannot move a layer behind the Background layer, nor can you move the Background layer forward.
Scale the thumbnails	To change the size of the thumbnails next to each layer name in the palette, choose Palette Options from the palette menu. Select a different radio button and press Return.

Getting rid of layers

You can delete the active layer from an image by choosing the Delete Layer command from the palette menu. Or you can simply drag the layer onto the trash icon in the bottom right corner of the Layers palette.

The problem with deleting a layer is that it gets rid of the image detail on that layer as well. If you want to delete the layer without deleting what's on it, you have to merge the layers. Photoshop takes stuff from multiple layers, puts it all on one layer, and throws the extra layers in the trash.

1. Hide all the layers that you don't want to merge. Make sure that all layers you do want to merge are visible.

   The best way to accomplish this is to Option-click on the eyeball in front of one of the layers you want to merge. This hides all but that one layer. Then click in the eyeball column in front of each of the other layers you want to merge, making them visible.

2. Choose the Merge Layers command from the Layers palette menu. Photoshop merges all visible layers onto a single layer.

3. To display the invisible layers — which remain independent layers — Option-click on the eyeball icon again.

If you want to merge *all* layers in the image, first make sure that all layers are visible. Then choose the Flatten Image command from the palette menu. If one or more layers are hidden, Photoshop displays a message asking you whether it's okay to discard the invisible layers. If this is not okay, press the Escape key or click on Cancel. Otherwise, press Return.

Masking layers

Photoshop provides three kinds of masks that you can apply to layers.

- The first mask, called the *transparency mask*, is created automatically. Some portions of the layer are transparent, some are opaque, and others are somewhere in between. This mask updates as you edit the image.

- If you add a *layer mask*, you can carve holes into a layer and make portions translucent without harming so much as a pixel of image detail in the layer.

- A *clipping group* combines a series of layers together and masks them using the transparency mask of the lowest layer in the group.

Because transparency masks happen automatically, you don't need to pay much attention to them. In fact, you can use them in only two ways:

Transparency Mask Trick	*How You Do It*
Paint inside the mask	Because Photoshop always knows which parts of the active layer are transparent and translucent, you can tell the program to protect those areas and keep them transparent and translucent. Just select the Preserve Transparency check box near the top of the Layers palette. To paint in any portion of the active layer, turn the Preserve Transparency check box off.
TIP Select the masked area	To convert the transparency mask for the active layer to a selection outline, press ⌘-Option-T. You can then apply the selection to a different layer by selecting that layer or use the selection outline in any other manner you see fit.

Layer masks and clipping groups are a little more involved. I explain how to create and edit layer masks in the following steps. After that, another set of steps walks you through the process of creating a clipping group.

Creating a layer mask

1. Click on the layer name that you want to edit in the Layers palette. Photoshop makes the layer active.
2. Choose the Add Layer Mask command from the palette menu. A second thumbnail appears to the left of the layer name. The thumbnail appears white, outlined by a thick border. The border shows that the layer mask is active.

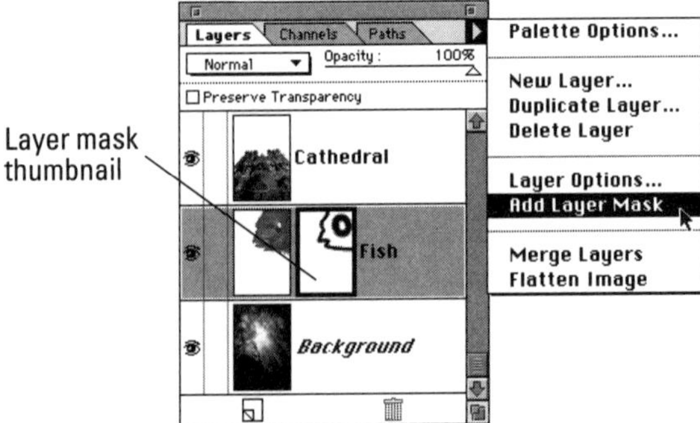

3. Press B to select the paintbrush tool. Then press D to change the foreground color to black.
4. Now paint in the image window. Notice how the layer becomes transparent as you paint?

   You're actually painting not on the layer, but on the layer mask. Where the layer mask is white — as it started out — the layer is fully visible. Where the layer mask is black — as in the brushstrokes — the layer becomes invisible.
5. Press E to select the eraser tool. Now erase some of the areas you just painted. Alternatively, you can press X to choose the default colors and continue painting with the paintbrush.

   The layer becomes visible again because you are painting with white.
6. To edit the layer instead of the mask, click on the left thumbnail, which represents the layer. Now if you paint, you change the layer, not the mask.

7. To turn the mask off, ⌘-click on the layer mask thumbnail. A red X covers the thumbnail, and all portions of the layer become visible again.

   To turn the mask back on, ⌘-click on the layer mask thumbnail again.

8. To view the layer mask by itself, Option-click on the layer mask thumbnail. Photoshop hides the image and displays the mask as a grayscale image.

   To view the image again, Option-click on any thumbnail in the Layers palette.

9. To delete the layer mask, choose the Remove Layer Mask command from the palette menu. Photoshop asks you whether you want to apply the layer mask to the layer — permanently altering the layer — or just throw the layer mask away. Click on the Apply button to apply the layer mask; click on the Discard button to throw it away.

Creating a clipping group

A clipping group is a group of layers that are masked by the transparency mask of the lowest layer. In other words, the transparent areas in the lowest layer are transparent throughout the group.

1. Decide which layers you want to group together. Then move them forward and backward until they're all next to each other.

2. Which layer contains the transparency mask that you want to use? Make that layer the lowest layer in the group.

   Suppose that you have two layers, one with a cathedral on it and one with a fish. If you want to paint the cathedral onto the fish, the fish should be in back of the cathedral.

3. Click on the top layer that you want to add to the group to make that layer active. Then choose the Layer Options command. After the dialog box appears, select the Group With Previous Layer check box and press Return.

   The horizontal line in the Layers palette between the active layer and the layer below it becomes dotted, showing that the two layers are part of the same group.

An easier way to group layers is to Option-click on the horizontal line between them. The cursor changes to two circles with a left-pointing arrowhead. Option-clicking on a horizontal line makes it dotted.

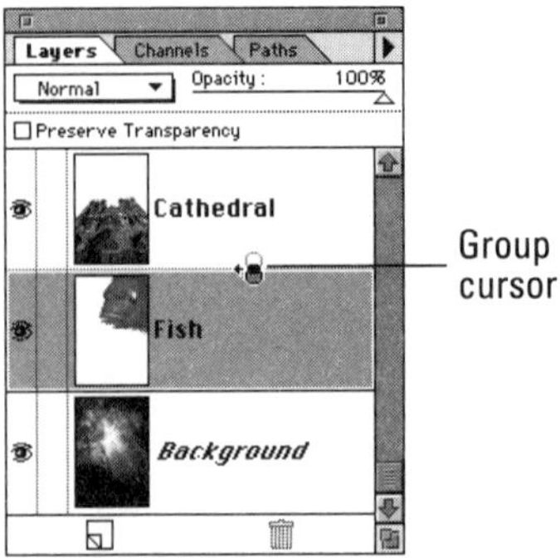

4. Option-click on the horizontal lines between the other layers you want to add to the group.
5. To remove a layer from the group, Option-click on the dotted horizontal line between that layer and the others in the group.

Blending layers

Another way to edit layers (and floating selections) without harming so much as a single pixel is to blend them together. For example, you can drag the Opacity slider triangle at the top of the Layers palette to make the active layer translucent. This lets you see through the active layer to the layers below.

You can change the Opacity of a layer from the keyboard when a selection or navigation tool is selected. (To be more precise, the shortcut works with the marquee, lasso, magic wand, move, hand, zoom, crop, type, and eyedropper tools.)

Just press a number key to change the Opacity of the active layer in 10 percent increments — 1 for 10 percent, 2 for 20 percent, all the way up to 0 for 100 percent.

You can also apply blend modes to layers and floating selections by choosing options from the pop-up menu in the upper left corner of the Layers palette. Though I already defined these modes in Part I, I hate to send you flipping through the book to find them. So here are the blend modes again, revised slightly to put them in context:

Blend Mode	*How It Works*
Normal	The Normal mode applies no special blending routine to the active layer.
Dissolve	When you choose this option, Photoshop changes the translucent areas of the active layer to a random scatter of pixels, creating a roughened effect.
Behind	This blend mode is available only when you're editing a floating selection on a layer. Choose the Behind option to position the floating selection behind the opaque pixels in the layer, as if it were actually on a lower layer.
Clear	Again, this option works only when you're editing a floating selection on a layer. Clear fills the selection with transparency, turning it into a movable hole. Try it out; it's kind of fun.
Multiply	This blend mode darkens the colors in the image, as if the active layer were printed on a piece of translucent film and tacked in front of the rest of the image.
Screen	Screen is Multiply's opposite. It lightens colors as if the active layer were a slide loaded into a projector and shined onto the rest of the image.
Overlay	This mode mixes the colors in the active layer with those in the rest of the image in fairly even increments, lightening the image only when the pixels in the active layer are lighter than those in the rest of the image and darkening it when the pixels are darker.
Soft Light	This is a wimpy version of Overlay that casts a soft glazing of the active layer over the rest of the image.

(continued)

Blend Mode	How It Works
Hard Light	Hard Light is the opposite of Overlay, which means that it favors the active layer over the image behind it. Use it when you want an effect somewhere between Normal and Overlay.
Darken	When Darken is selected, a pixel in the active layer is visible only if it is darker than the pixel behind it. Lighter pixels are transparent.
Lighten	With this option, a pixel in the active layer is visible only if it is lighter than the pixel behind it. Darker pixels are transparent.
Difference	This option inverts the image according to the colors in the active layer. Dark colors in the active layer have little effect, but light colors turn the image into a photo-negative.
Hue	The Hue blend mode applies the hue of the active layer but retains the saturation and luminosity of the background image.
Saturation	This mode applies the saturation of the active layer to the hues and luminosities in the image behind the layer.
Color	The Color mode applies both the hue and saturation of the active layer but keeps the luminosity of the background image.
Luminosity	This option leaves the hues and saturation levels of the background image unscathed and applies the luminosity of the active layer. Though Luminosity is the last blend mode in the pop-up menu, it's the first one you'll want to try. It almost always produces pleasing results when applied to a layer.

Chapter 18 in *Photoshop 3 For Macs For Dummies* shows how to create a surrealistic composition using the Normal, Multiply, Screen, Hard Light, and Luminosity modes.

The Options Palette

The Options palette lets you modify the performance of the tools in the toolbox. Only two tools — the move and type tools — cannot be modified from this palette.

To display the Options palette, choose Window⇨Palettes⇨Show Options or just press the Return key. You can also double-click on a tool icon in the toolbox.

Because the options and even the title of the Options palette change according to which tool is selected, I explain each and every variation on the palette in Part I. However, the two palette commands remain constant regardless of the tool.

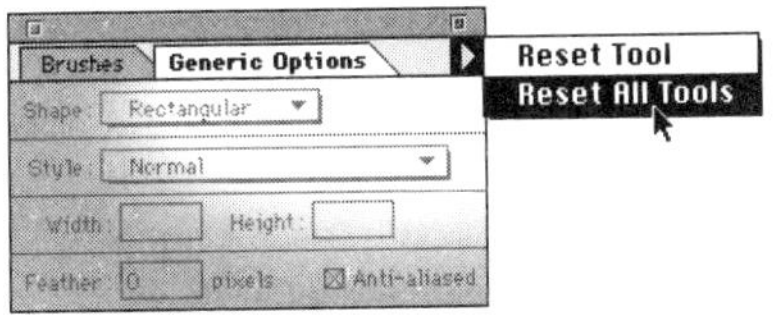

Options Palette Command	What It Does
Reset Tool	This command restores the options for the selected tool to the original default settings. An alert message appears to confirm your request.
Reset All Tools	Choose this command to restore the options for *all* tools to the default settings.

When you press the Return key when the marquee or lasso tool is selected, Photoshop not only displays the appropriate Options palette, it also highlights the Feather value. If the magic wand or paint bucket tool is selected, Photoshop highlights the Tolerance value. If the line tool is selected, it highlights the Line Width value. In any case, just type a new value and press Return to change it.

You can also change a highlighted value in a Photoshop option box — like Feather or Tolerance — by pressing the up or down arrow key. Press the up arrow key to raise the value by 1; press the down arrow key to lower the value by 1. You can also raise or lower the highlighted value by 10 by pressing Shift-up arrow or Shift-down arrow.

The Paths Palette

Photoshop's Paths palette gives you an alternative method for selecting part of an image. Rather than dragging inside an image to create a selection outline, as you do with the lasso tool, you use the tools in the Paths palette to draw free-form selection outlines known as *paths.* To create a path, you position individual points and adjust the curvature of the segments between those points by dragging control handles. It's sort of like drawing a dot-to-dot outline around the detail you want to select.

The Paths palette is actually a combination toolbox and palette. You draw and modify paths using the tools along the top of the palette. Then you name and organize the paths much as you name and organize masks and layers in the Channels and Layers palettes.

Although they're rather laborious to use, paths are highly accurate, and you can edit them long after you create them.

To display the Paths palette, choose Window⇨Palettes⇨Show Paths. Choose Window⇨Palettes⇨Hide Paths to hide the palette.

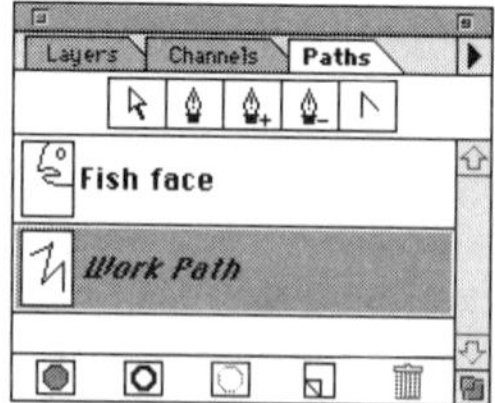

You can also display the Paths palette by pressing T. This selects the pen tool, which is the second tool inside the palette.

Using the path tools

The following list identifies the tools in the Paths palette and explains how to use them:

Paths Palette Tool	How It Works
Arrow tool	This tools lets you drag points and control handles to reshape a path.
	You can access the arrow tool by pressing and holding the ⌘ key. Or press T when the pen tool is selected to switch to the arrow tool. (Pressing T again returns to the pen tool.)
Pen tool	Use the pen tool to draw paths in Photoshop one point at a time. I explain this tool in more detail in the next list.
Insert point tool	Click on an existing path to add a point to it.
	You can access this function when the arrow tool is selected by ⌘-Option-clicking on a segment in a path. If the pen tool is selected, Control-click.
Remove point tool	Click on a point in a path to delete the point without creating a break in the outline of the path.
	To accomplish this when the arrow tool is selected, ⌘-Option-click on a point. When the pen tool is selected, Control-click.
Convert point	Click or drag on a point with this tool to convert the point to a corner or smooth point. You can also drag on a control handle to convert the point.
	Press the Control key to access the convert point tool when the arrow is selected. Press ⌘ and Control when the pen tool is selected.

Using the pen tool

When drawing with the pen tool, you build a path by creating individual points. Photoshop automatically connects the points with straight or curved segments. You can adjust the curvature of each segment by moving the control handle in relation to the segment. You bend and tug at the curved segment as if it were a piece of soft wire.

Here's how to use the pen tool to create paths in Photoshop:

Pen Tool Operation	*How You Do It*
Build a path	To build a path, create one point after another until the path is the desired length and shape. Photoshop automatically draws a segment between each new point and its predecessor.
Create a corner point	Click with the pen tool to create a corner point, which represents the corner between two straight segments in a path.
Create a smooth point	Drag with the pen tool to create a smooth point with two symmetrical control handles. A smooth point ensures that one segment meets with another in a continuous arc.
Create a cusp point	After creating a smooth point, Option-drag from the point you just created to redirect a control handle. The result is a cusp point, which represents the corner between two curved segments.
Close the path	If you plan on eventually converting the path to a selection outline, you need to complete the outline by clicking again on the first point in the path. Such a path is called a *closed path* because it forms one continuous outline.
Extend an open path	To reactivate an open path, click or drag on one of its endpoints. Photoshop draws a segment between the endpoint and the next point you create.

Pen Tool Operation	How You Do It
Join two open paths	To join one open path with another open path, click or drag on an endpoint in the first path and then click or drag on an endpoint in the second.

Other path stuff

Photoshop automatically adds an item named *Work Path* to the Paths palette as you create a new path. The only problem is, the program adds every new path you create to this same item. If you want to name and store the paths separately, you have to engage in a little hands-on organization.

The following list explains the different ways to organize paths and apply them to an image, whether as lines, shapes, or selection outlines.

Paths Palette Operation	How You Do It
Name a path	To name a path and store it along with the image, choose the Save Path command from the palette menu. Or just double-click on the *Work Path* item. A dialog box appears, asking you to name the path. Enter a name and press Return.
	To skip the dialog box and have Photoshop name the path automatically, press Option when choosing the Save Path command. Or drag the *Work Path* item onto the new path icon at the bottom of the palette.

(continued)

Paths Palette Operation	How You Do It

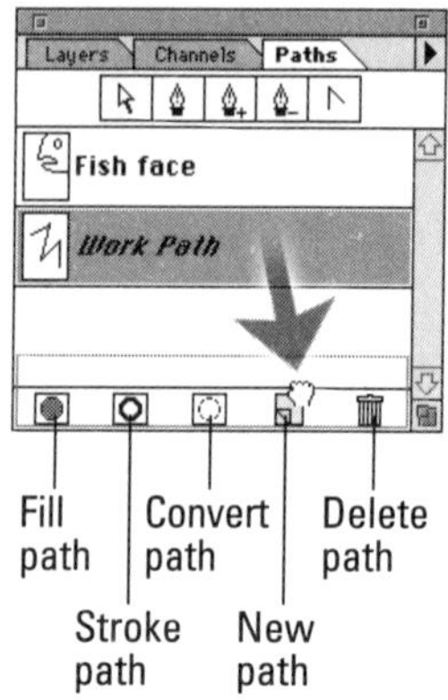

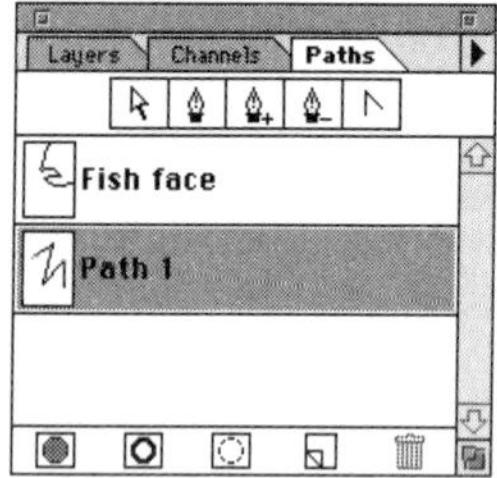

Paths Palette Operation	How You Do It
Deactivate a path	To hide a path and make it inactive, choose the Turn Off Path command from the Paths palette menu. The path is no longer visible in the image window.
	You can also deactivate a path by clicking in the empty space between the path names and the icons in the palette. Or just Shift-click on the active path name.
Activate a path	To activate a path, click on its name in the Paths palette. The path is again visible in the image window.

Paths Palette Operation	How You Do It
Create a new path	To start a new path under a different name, deactivate all paths and then start clicking and dragging with the pen tool.
	Or, if you prefer, choose the New Path command from the palette menu — or click on the new path icon at the bottom of the palette — to create a new named path.
	If you deactivate the *Work Path* item without naming it and then start creating a new path, Photoshop deletes the old unnamed path. So be sure to name the *Work Path* item before deactivating it.
Duplicate a path	To make a copy of the active path, choose the Duplicate Path command from the palette menu. Or drag the path name onto the new path icon at the bottom of the palette.
Convert a path to a selection	To convert the active path to a selection outline, choose the Mask Selection command from the palette menu or click on the convert path icon — the dotted circle smack dab in the center of the icons at the bottom of the palette.
	If you choose the command, Photoshop displays a dialog box asking you whether you want to feather the selection outline and add it or subtract it from any existing selection in the image.
	You can accomplish several of these tasks without entering the dialog box. To add the path to an existing selection, Shift-click on the convert path icon. To subtract the path, ⌘-click on the icon. To find the intersection of path and selection, ⌘-Shift-click on the icon.

(continued)

Paths Palette Operation	How You Do It
	For the best results, hide the path after converting it to a selection by Shift-clicking on the path name. This way, the path won't interfere with your editing.
	Simpler still, just select one of the selection or navigation tools and press the Enter key. This converts the active path to a selection and hides the path with one keystroke.
Convert a selection to a path	Just as you can create a selection from a path, you can create a path from a selection. First, make sure that no path is active. Then click on the convert path icon. The new path appears as an unnamed *Work Path* in the palette.
Fill a path	To fill the active path with the foreground color, click on the fill path icon in the bottom left corner of the palette.
	You can also choose the Fill path command from the palette menu, which displays a dialog box. For information about the options in this dialog box, see "Edit⇨Fill" in Part III.
Trace a path	Photoshop will automatically trace around a path with any one of the painting or editing tools. This is one of my favorite path functions.
	To trace along the outline of the active path, choose the Stroke Path command from the palette menu. A dialog box appears, sporting one pop-up menu. Select the tool you want Photoshop to trace with and press Return.

Paths Palette Operation	*How You Do It*
TIP	Easier still, select the tool with which you want to trace in the toolbox. Then click on the stroke path icon at the bottom of the palette — the one that looks like a thickly outlined circle. Or just press the Enter key.
Delete a path	To delete the active path, choose the Delete Path command from the palette menu. Or drag the path name onto the trash icon in the bottom right corner of the palette.
Scale the thumbnails	As you can in the Channels and Layers palettes, you can change the size of the thumbnails next to each path name in the palette. Just choose Palette Options from the palette menu, select a different radio button, and press Return.

Part III

The Photoshop Menu

Basic Menu Stuff

Photoshop provides seven menus of commands — File, Edit, Mode, Image, Filter, Select, and Window. Click and hold on any menu name to display a list of commands. Choose a command by dragging over the command name and releasing the mouse button.

If a command name includes an ellipsis (. . .) — such as File⇨Open . . . — the command displays a dialog box filled with options. These options work as follows:

Type of Option	*How You Use It*
☒ Check box	Click on a check box to turn it on or off. When on, the check box has an X in it. When off, it looks like an empty square. You can select as many check boxes in a group as you like.
◉ Radio button	Again, click on a circular radio button to turn it on or off. When on, the radio button has a black dot in it. When off, the circle is empty. You can select only one radio button in each group of radio buttons.
Pop ▾ Pop-up menu	Click and hold on a pop-up menu to display a menu of options. Drag to the option you want to select and release the mouse button.
100 Option box	Option boxes contain numerical values. To change the value in an option box, drag over the value to highlight it, and then enter a new value.
TIP	Pressing the Tab key highlights the contents of the next option box in a dialog box. Pressing Shift-Tab highlights the value in the previous option box.
	You can nudge a highlighted value from the keyboard by pressing the up or down arrow key. Press the up arrow key to raise the value by 1; press the down arrow key to lower the value by 1.

(continued)

Type of Option	*How You Use It*
	You can also raise or lower the highlighted value by 10 by pressing Shift-up arrow or Shift-down arrow.
OK Button	Click on a button to leave a dialog box or enter a different dialog box. For example, clicking on the OK button closes the dialog box and applies the command to the image; clicking on Cancel closes the dialog box and cancels the command.
	If a button is surrounded by a heavy outline — like the OK button — you can activate it by pressing the Return or Enter key. Press ⌘-period or Escape to activate the Cancel button.

If a command name does not include an ellipsis, Photoshop generally applies it with no questions asked. Every once in a while, the program might ask some small question — "Do you want to save the file before closing it?" — but it doesn't bother you with a big, confusing dialog box.

The sections in Part III are organized alphabetically by menu. For example, the Copy command is explained in "Edit⇨Copy." Commands under submenus are grouped by submenu. For example, Filter⇨Sharpen⇨Unsharp Mask is explained in "Filter⇨Sharpen."

Edit⇨Clear

The Edit⇨Clear command either deletes a selected area or fills it with the background color, depending on whether the selection is floating and which layer it's on:

- If the selection is floating, the Clear command simply deletes it.
- If the selection is not floating and it's on the Background layer, Edit⇨Clear fills the selection with white.
- If the selection is not floating and it's on any layer except Background, the Clear command makes the selection transparent, so you can see through to lower layers.

Unless the selection is floating, the selection outline remains intact after you choose Clear. If nothing is selected, the Clear command is dimmed.

A quick way to choose the Clear command is to just press Delete.

Edit⇨Copy

Choose the Copy command to duplicate the selected area of an image and send it to the Macintosh Clipboard. The Clipboard is a portion of your computer's memory that's set aside to hold one thing at a time. When you choose Copy, you put the selection in the Clipboard and delete the old Clipboard contents.

You can also use the Copy command to copy text inside the Type Tool dialog box (discussed in "The Type Tool" in Part I).

Press ⌘-C to choose the Copy command in any Macintosh program, including Photoshop.

The Copy command is dimmed if nothing in the image is selected.

Edit⇨Create Publisher

Under System 7.0 and later, Photoshop allows you to "publish" an image to disk. The published file is called an *edition*. You can then "subscribe" to the edition inside another program.

The system software creates a live link between Photoshop, the edition on disk, and the subscriber program so that any changes made in Photoshop are reflected in the subscriber program as well.

For example, suppose that you publish the image of a girl's face in Photoshop. Then you subscribe to the edition inside Microsoft Word. Three weeks later, you decide to paint a mustache on the girl. The next time you open your Word document, Word automatically imports the newest version of the girl, mustache and all.

Follow these steps to publish an image:

1. Make sure that the image is deselected by choosing Select⇨None or pressing ⌘-D. Photoshop will not publish a selected image.
2. Choose Edit⇨Create Publisher, which brings up a dialog box that lets you name and locate the edition on disk.

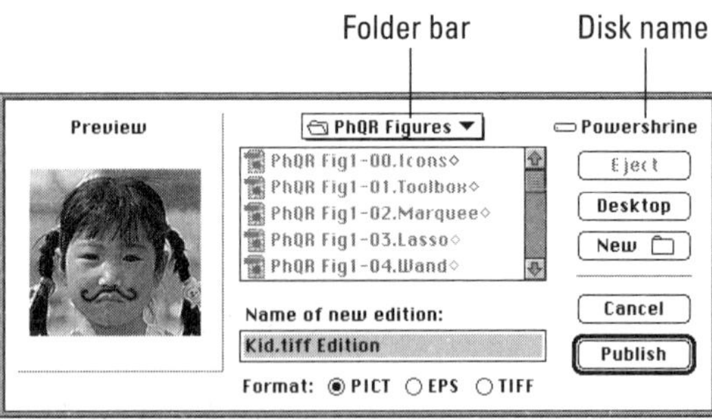

3. Use the navigation controls to figure out where you want to put the edition. The current folder is always listed in the folder bar above the scrolling list. The dimmed items in the list are files inside the current folder.

   - Click on the Desktop button (or press ⌘-D) to go to the desktop level, which is the lowest level in the folder hierarchy. If the Macintosh used real folders, the desktop level would be the file cabinet.
   - Double-click on a folder in the scrolling list to enter that folder.
   - Click on the disk name in the upper right corner of the dialog box to exit the current folder.
   - You can also drag from the folder bar to see a pop-up menu of the folders that contain the current folder. Select a folder to move to it.
   - Click on the New Folder button (or press ⌘-N) to create a new folder inside the current folder. An option box appears, asking you to name the new folder. Enter a name and press Return.

4. Select one of the Format radio buttons to specify which file format Photoshop should save the edition in.

   The best choice for editions is PICT because this is the system software's native format. But you can also choose TIFF or EPS if you know the subscriber program supports one of those formats.

   For more information about file formats, see "File⇨Save" later in Part III.

5. Enter the name of the edition into the Name of New Edition option box. The name can be up to 31 characters long.

6. Click on the Publish button or press Return. Photoshop saves the edition to disk as instructed.

From now on, Photoshop will update the edition each time you save the image using File⇨Save.

As I already mentioned, the Create Publisher command is dimmed if any part of the image is selected. But it is also dimmed if the image has already been published (in which case you would instead choose Edit⇨Publisher Options to modify the settings).

Unlike most programs, Photoshop does not let you subscribe to edition files. You can only publish them.

Edit⇨Crop

The Crop command is an alternative to the crop tool (described in "The Crop Tool" in Part I). Like the tool, the Crop command clips an image down to a smaller size by throwing out extraneous detail.

To use this command, use the rectangular marquee tool to select the portion of the image you want to retain. (You can use other tools if you like, but the selection must be exactly rectangular or the Crop command is dimmed.) Then choose Edit⇨Crop. Photoshop clips away everything outside the marquee.

Always exercise caution when cropping. Make sure that you want to throw away the excess imagery before you choose Edit⇨Crop.

Edit⇨Cut

The Cut command deletes the selected area from an image and sends it to the Clipboard. Inside the Type Tool dialog box, Edit⇨Cut deletes the highlighted text and sends it to the Clipboard. Either way, the Cut command displaces the previous contents of the Clipboard.

The keyboard combination ⌘-X is the universal shortcut for the Cut command throughout all Macintosh programs.

As with Edit⇨Copy, the Cut command is dimmed if nothing in the image is selected.

Edit⇨Define Pattern

As I mentioned in "The Rubber Stamp Tool" in Part I, you can paint with a pattern using the rubber stamp tool. You can also fill a selected area with a pattern using Edit⇨Fill (as explained later in Part III).

But before you can use either of these options, you have to define the pattern using Edit⇨Define Pattern:

1. Select the area that you want to use as a pattern.
2. Choose Edit⇨Define Pattern.

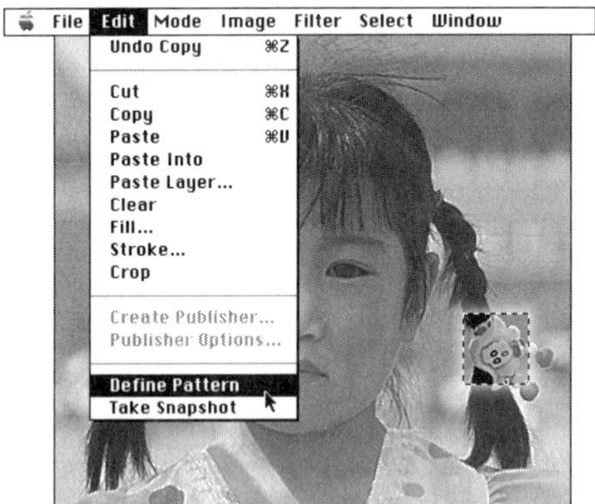

3. Now apply the pattern. For example, you could double-click on the rubber stamp tool icon in the toolbox, select Pattern (Aligned) from the Option pop-up menu in the Rubber Stamp Options palette, and then drag inside the image. Photoshop repeats the pattern over and over again as you paint.

Edit⇨Define Pattern is dimmed if nothing is selected. Also, keep in mind that Photoshop only remembers one pattern at a time. So by choosing Define Pattern, you get rid of the previous pattern.

Edit⇨Fill

Edit⇨Fill is one of my favorite commands in Photoshop. It lets you fill a selected area with a solid color, a pattern, or even with the saved image or snapshot.

1. Select an area in your image. If you don't select anything, Edit⇨Fill fills the entire image.
2. Choose Edit⇨Fill. The Fill dialog box appears.

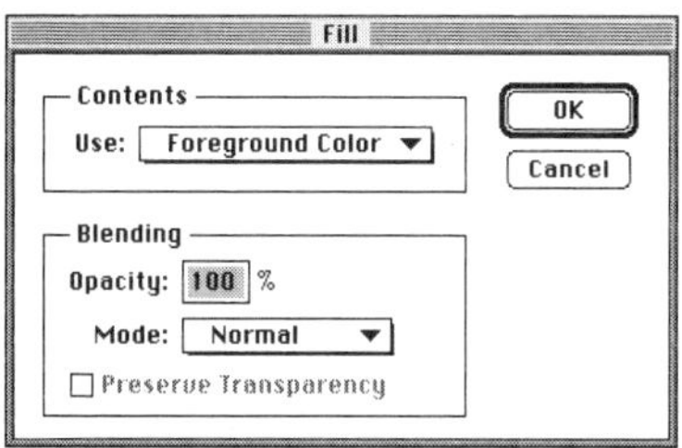

3. In the Use pop-up menu, choose the stuff that you want to use to fill the selection (or image).
   - Choose the Foreground Color option to fill the selection with the foreground color. Choose Background Color to fill the selection with the background color.

- The Pattern option fills the selection with the pattern you defined using Edit⇨Define Pattern (as explained earlier in Part III).
- Choose the Saved option to fill the selection with the corresponding portion of the image saved to disk. It's like reverting the selection to its appearance when last saved.
- The Snapshot option restores the selection to the way it looked when you last chose Edit⇨Take Snapshot (as explained later in Part III).
- The remaining options fill the selection with a flat color — either Black, 50% Gray, or White.

4. You can blend the fill with the pixels inside the selection by changing the Opacity value. Lower values result in a more translucent fill.
5. Choose an option from the Mode pop-up menu to mix the fill colors with the pixels in the selection using Photoshop's hefty supply of blend modes. For an overview of how these options work, see the "Blending layers" section of "The Layers Palette" in Part II.
6. Select the Preserve Transparency check box to fill only the opaque portions of a layer and leave the transparent portions untouched. This option is dimmed when you are working on the Background layer.
7. Click on the OK button or press Return to apply the fill.

Photoshop offers three shortcuts for filling selections:

- To fill a nonfloating selection on the Background layer with the background color, press Delete.
- To fill any selection with the foreground color, press Option-Delete.
- To bring up the Fill dialog box, press Shift-Delete.

Edit⇨Paste

After using Edit⇨Copy or Edit⇨Cut to transfer a selection to the Macintosh Clipboard, you can retrieve the image by choosing Edit⇨Paste. This command pastes a copy of the contents of the Clipboard. The contents remain intact, so you can paste an image several times in a row to make multiple copies of an image.

The Paste command pastes its cargo directly in the center of the image. If part of the image is selected, Photoshop pastes the image smack dab in the center of the selection. The pasted stuff floats above the surface of the image so that you can move it around without harming the image below.

If you copied or cut some text inside the Type Tool dialog box, you can retrieve the text by choosing Edit⇨Paste. However, you can't paste text outside the Type Tool dialog box, and you can't paste an image inside the dialog box.

In all Macintosh programs, pressing ⌘-V is the same as choosing Edit⇨Paste.

The Paste command is dimmed if the Clipboard is empty or if it contains stuff that you can't paste into Photoshop.

Edit⇨Paste Into

The Paste Into command pastes an image inside the selection. You can move the pasted image around inside the selection without ever harming the deselected pixels.

Older versions of Photoshop contain a Paste Behind command, which lets you paste an image behind the selection. Just the opposite of the Paste Into command, Paste Behind protects the selected pixels and pastes the image inside the deselected areas. In Photoshop 3, you can achieve this same effect by pressing the Option key when choosing Edit⇨Paste Into.

Edit⇨Paste Into is dimmed if the Clipboard is empty or if no portion of the image is selected.

Edit⇨Paste Layer

This command pastes the contents of the Clipboard onto a new layer.

Frankly, it's easier to establish a new layer by dragging and dropping a selection from another image or by floating a selection and converting it into a layer. See "The Layers Palette" in Part II for the whole story.

Edit⇨Paste Layer is dimmed if the Clipboard is empty.

Edit⇨Publisher Options

After publishing an image to disk using Edit⇨Create Publisher (as described earlier in Part III), you can modify the publisher settings by choosing Edit⇨Publisher Options:

1. Choose the Publisher Options command to display a dialog box of standardized Macintosh publishing options.

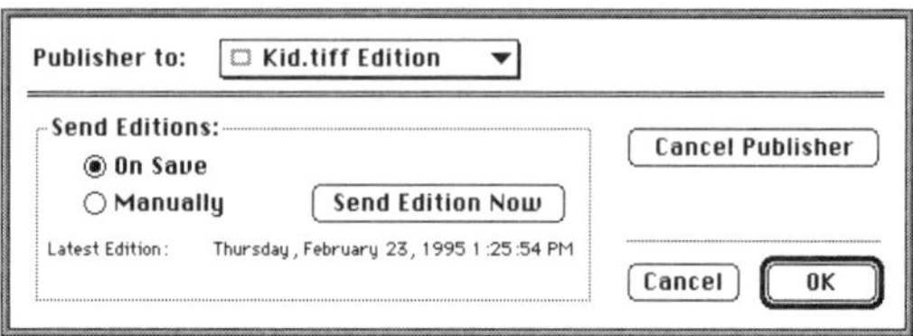

2. If you're curious about where the edition file is located on disk, click and hold on the Publisher To pop-up menu. The menu lists the entire folder hierarchy. You can't choose anything; you can only look at it.
3. By default, Photoshop automatically updates the edition file every time you save the image using File⇨Save. If you prefer to save updates to the edition file manually, select the Manually radio button.

   From now on, you'll have to choose Edit⇨Publisher Options and click on the Send Edition Now button to save the edition file to disk. (To instruct Photoshop to update the edition automatically again, select the On Save radio button.)
4. If you want to get rid of the edition file, click on the Cancel Publisher button. When Photoshop asks you to confirm your request, click on the Yes button. Photoshop closes the dialog box and breaks the link to the Edition file. The next time you save the image, Photoshop deletes the edition file from disk.

   If you don't want to delete the edition, just click on the OK button or press Return to confirm your settings and close the dialog box.

The Publisher Option command is dimmed if the image has not yet been published using Edit⇨Create Publisher.

Edit⇨Stroke

The Stroke command traces a border around the edges of a selection. The border is always colored with the foreground color.

Unlike the Stroke command in the Paths palette menu (discussed in "The Paths Palette" in Part II), Edit⇨Stroke does not trace the border using a painting or editing tool. Instead, Photoshop draws a smooth border of a specified thickness.

1. Select the portion of the image you want to stroke.
2. Set the foreground color to the color you want to apply to the stroke.
3. Choose Edit⇨Stroke to display the Stroke dialog box.

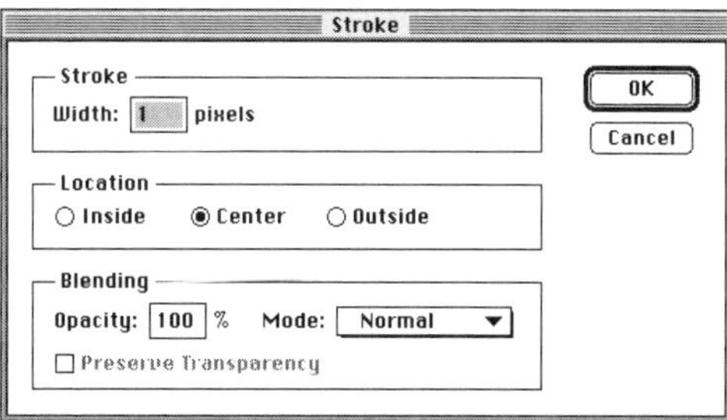

4. Enter the thickness of the border into the Width option box. The value is measured in pixels.
5. Select a Location radio button to determine how the border rides the selection outline.
   - Select Inside to draw the border fully inside the selection outline.
   - Select the Outside radio button to draw the border completely outside the selection.
   - If you click on Center, the border sits astride the selection outline, half inside the selection and half outside.
6. You can blend the stroke with the existing pixels in the image by changing the Opacity value. Lower values result in a more translucent border.

7. Choose an option from the Mode pop-up menu to mix the foreground color with the pixels in the image using a blend mode. For an overview of how the Mode options work, see the "Selecting a blend mode" section of "The Fill Tools: Paint Bucket and Gradient" in Part I.
8. Select the Preserve Transparency check box to draw the border inside the opaque portions of a layer and leave the transparent portions unstroked. This option is dimmed when you're working on the Background layer.
9. Click on the OK button or press Return to draw the border around the selection.

If a selection is floating, Edit⇨Stroke defloats it. This means that the selection is adhered to the image. If you try to move a selection after floating it, you'll leave a background-colored hole. So be sure that you have positioned a selection properly before choosing the Stroke command.

The Stroke command is dimmed if no portion of the image is selected.

Edit⇨Take Snapshot

Choose the Take Snapshot command to store the selected portion of the image in memory. If no portion of the image is selected, Photoshop stores the entire image.

The purpose of the Snapshot command is to temporarily save an image in case you want to come back to it later. For example, if you want to produce an effect that requires several steps, but you're not sure whether you'll like the effect or not, choose Edit⇨Take Snapshot to serve as a safety net.

You can retrieve the snapshot using the rubber stamp tool (as explained in "The Rubber Stamp Tool" in Part I) or with Edit⇨Fill (described earlier in Part III).

Edit⇨Undo

Nearly all Macintosh programs offer an Undo command. Choose Edit⇨Undo to undo the last significant operation. Photoshop lists the last operation next to the Undo command so that you know what effect the command will have. For example, after you paint with the paintbrush, the command reads Undo Paintbrush.

After you choose Edit⇨Undo, the command changes to Redo, permitting you to reapply the operation. In other words, Redo undoes Undo.

The Print command has no effect on the Undo command. Therefore, you can apply an operation, print the image, and then undo the operation, just as if you had never issued the Print command. This means that you can adjust an image, print it to see how it looks, and undo the adjustment if you don't like it.

Be careful, however: Photoshop remembers your changes inside the Page Setup dialog box and lets you undo them. So don't choose Page Setup before Print if you want to undo a brushstroke or other operation after printing the image.

You can choose either the Undo or Redo command from the keyboard by pressing ⌘-Z.

The Undo command is dimmed if you haven't yet performed any operations on the open image or if Photoshop won't let you undo the last operation. Just to make sure everything's crystal clear, Photoshop even changes the command name to Can't Undo.

- You can't undo the File⇨Save and File⇨Save As commands. Not only do these commands render the Undo command null and void, they make it impossible to undo the operation you performed before choosing them.
- You can't undo the Quit command. There's a surprise. Also, when you relaunch Photoshop, it has no idea what you did during the previous session, so you can't undo the last changes you made before quitting.
- You can't undo changing a foreground or background color, adjusting a setting using one of the commands under the File⇨Preferences submenu, hiding or displaying palettes, changing a palette setting, or selecting a tool.

File⇨Acquire

The commands in the File⇨Acquire submenu allow you to open images stored on disk. You can also import images that you capture using scanning hardware hooked up to your computer.

The File⇨Open command — discussed later in Part III — also lets you open images stored on disk. So what's the difference between Open and Acquire? The Open command is built into Photoshop. The commands under the File⇨Acquire submenu are external modules that Photoshop loads into memory when you start up the program.

If you look inside the folder that contains the Photoshop program, you'll find a folder called Plug-Ins. Open this folder and you'll find another folder called Acquire/Export. Every one of the files in the Acquire/Export folder is an external module that shows up as a command in the File⇨Acquire or File⇨Export submenu.

You can add more modules to the Acquire/Export folder. For example, if you purchase a scanner to create digital photographs, it will undoubtedly include a module that shows up as a command in the File⇨Acquire submenu. This way, you can scan the image directly into Photoshop and start editing away.

Here's a list of the commands that are certain to show up in the File⇨Acquire submenu. Your submenu may include additional commands, but the following are the only ones that come with Photoshop.

Acquire Command	*What It Does*
Antialiased PICT	Use this command to open PICT files created in drawing programs such as Canvas, MacDraw, or Claris Draw. After you select the file you want to open, Photoshop asks you to enter the size of the file in pixels. Any size is acceptable, but bigger sizes produce better results.
PICT Resource	This command lets you open images stored inside the Macintosh Scrapbook. Just open the Scrapbook File inside the System Folder. Then use the arrow buttons to cycle through the images inside the Scrapbook.
QuickEdit	The QuickEdit command lets you open small parts of very large images that you may not be able to open all at once. Unfortunately, the command opens images saved in Photoshop 2.0, Scitex CT, and uncompressed TIFF formats only.

Acquire Command	*What It Does*
	After you select the image you want to open, Photoshop displays a preview of the image. Marquee the portion of the image you want to edit and press Return.
TWAIN Acquire	Choose this command to scan an image in from a TWAIN-compatible scanner. Note that most scanners are *not* TWAIN compatible, so this command is rarely useful. Consult the instructions provided with your scanner for complete information.
TWAIN Select Source	This command lets you set up your TWAIN-compatible scanner for use with Photoshop. You only need to perform this step the first time you use the scanner.

As you can see, these aren't the most useful commands in the world — particularly the two TWAIN commands — but you never know when they might come in handy.

File⇨Close

Choose File⇨Close to close the image you're working on. If you've made any changes to the image since the last time you saved it to disk, Photoshop asks whether you want to save those changes.

- Press Return to save the changes.
- Click on the Don't Save button or press D to abandon the changes.
- Click on the Cancel button or press Escape to cancel the Close command and return to the image window.

You can close an image by pressing ⌘-W. Or click inside the close box on the far left side of the title bar.

File⇨Export

The File⇨Export submenu provides commands that let you save an image or some part of an image in an unusual format. One of the commands even lets you print an image.

As with the File⇨Acquire commands, the Export commands are external modules stored in the Acquire/Export folder inside the Plug-Ins folder.

Your File⇨Export submenu may offer more commands than the four listed below. But the ones in this list are the only ones that come with Photoshop.

Export Command	*What It Does*
Amiga HAM	This command saves the image to the HAM format for use on Commodore Amiga computers. Unfortunately, HAM images have to conform to certain file sizes, which frequently results in squishing or stretching an image. Unless you use an Amiga, steer clear of this command.
ImageWriter Color	Choose this command to print a color image to an ImageWriter II printer with a color ribbon. After making some calculations, Photoshop displays a standard Page Setup dialog box and then prints away. (The Page Setup dialog box is explained in the "File⇨Page Setup" section later in Part III.)
Paths to Illustrator	If your image contains paths created using the pen tool in the Paths palette (explained in Part II), you can save them for use in Adobe Illustrator by choosing File⇨Export⇨Paths to Illustrator. You have the option of saving all paths, just one named set of paths, or the boundaries of the image.
Quick Edit Save	After opening a portion of an image using File⇨Acquire⇨Quick Edit (as described earlier in Part III), you can save the detail back to the original image by choosing File⇨Export⇨Quick Edit Save.

File⇨File Info

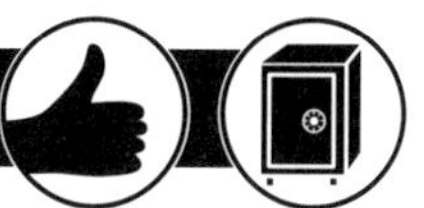

If you intend to distribute your images over on-line services or other means, you can attach information to them using File⇨File Info. You can enter captions, credits, and other explanatory information that other Photoshop users can view by simply choosing File⇨File Info.

When you choose the File Info command, Photoshop displays the File Info dialog box, which contains five panels of options. To change panels, choose an option from the Section pop-up menu. You can also press the keyboard shortcuts — ⌘-1 through ⌘-5, one for each panel — or click on the Next button to advance from one panel to another.

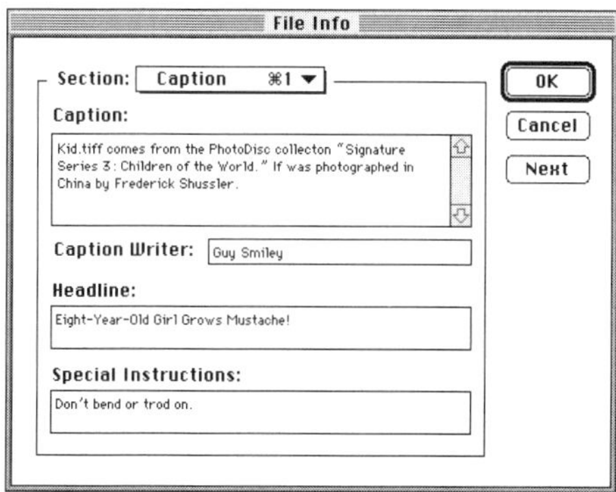

File Info Panel	*What It's For*
Caption	Enter a description of the image in the Caption option box, which can hold up to 2,000 characters. You can also enter a headline for the caption, a credit, and instructions. You can print the contents of the Caption option box along with the image by choosing File⇨Page Setup and selecting the Caption check box.

(continued)

File Info Panel	What It's For
Keyword	Click on the Add button to create keywords that can be used in searches. This feature is especially useful if the image will be included in a large electronic library.
Categories	Provided specifically for use with news services agencies, the Categories panel enables you to organize images into news and features categories.
Credits	Enter the photographer and other credit information into the option boxes in the Credits panel.
Origin	This panel tells where the image comes from — the city, state, date of creation, and so forth. Again, this information is useful if the image will be included in an electronic library.

You don't have to fill out every option box in every panel. In fact, you may want to limit yourself to the Caption panel. The information in the credits panel is the least likely to be ignored because it's the first panel to appear when you choose File⇨File Info.

File⇨New

Choose File⇨New to create a brand new image inside Photoshop. You'll probably work most frequently with scanned photographs that you open using File⇨Open. But the New command comes in handy when you want to paint something from scratch and when you want to copy part of an image and paste it into a new image window.

1. Choose File⇨New to display the New dialog box.
2. Change the Width and Height values to specify the size of the canvas on which you'll create your new image. You can change the units of measurement by selecting options from the pop-up menus to the right of the option boxes.

   The Width pop-up menu offers an unusual option called Columns, which allows you to precisely match the width of an image to the columns in a printed document created in

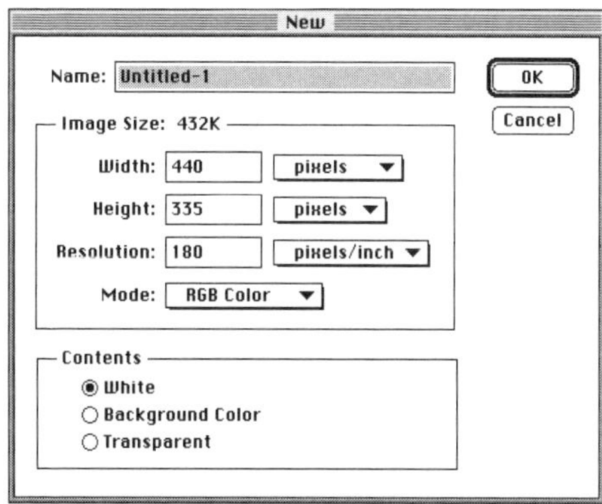

PageMaker or QuarkXPress. Specify the size of your columns by choosing File⇨Preferences⇨Units and entering values into the Column Size option boxes.

3. Enter the number of pixels that print in an inch into the Resolution option box.

   - If you specified the Width or Height value in any unit except Pixels, the Resolution value changes the number of pixels packed into the image. (A high Resolution value results in more pixels.)
   - If the Width and Height values are set to Pixels, the Resolution setting affects printing only; it has no effect on the number of pixels in the image.

   Either way, Photoshop makes no attempt to display the specified number of pixels per inch on-screen. The 100 percent view size shows one image pixel per every screen pixel regardless of Resolution setting.

Don't fret if you're not sure about the exact size and resolution settings you want to use. You can always change these settings later on down the line using Image⇨Canvas Size and Image⇨Image Size.

4. Select a color mode from the Mode pop-up menu. If you want to create a color image, you'll generally want to select RGB. If you don't want color, select Grayscale.

5. Select a Contents radio button to specify the color with which Photoshop should fill the new image.

   - White fills the image with white.

- The Background Color option fills the new image with the current background color.
- The Transparent option turns the new image into a floating layer filled with no color at all. When the image window comes up on-screen, this transparency is represented by a gray checkerboard pattern.

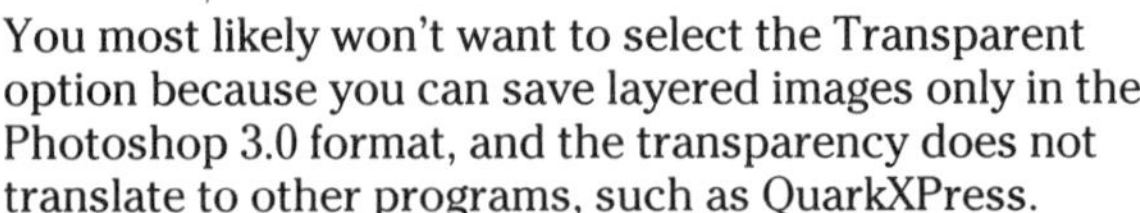

You most likely won't want to select the Transparent option because you can save layered images only in the Photoshop 3.0 format, and the transparency does not translate to other programs, such as QuarkXPress.

6. You can name the image by entering a name into the Name option box. Don't worry if you aren't certain how you want to name it yet. You can always change the name when you save the image to disk using File⇨Save.
7. Click on the OK button or press Return to create the new image window.

If you have copied anything to the Clipboard, the Width, Height, and Resolution values as well as the Mode setting conform exactly to the Clipboard's contents. You can make an image match the settings of another open image by choosing a file name from the bottom of the Window menu while inside the New dialog box. Amazing, huh?

To choose the New command from the keyboard, press ⌘-N.

File⇨Open

Use File⇨Open to open an image stored on disk. The image might be a scan saved in the TIFF format, or it might be an image from a Photo CD. It can even be an EPS drawing created in Illustrator. If it's a photograph or graphic, Photoshop stands a better-than-even chance of being able to open it.

1. Choose File⇨Open to bring up a dialog box that enables you to locate images on disk.
2. Use the Desktop button, folder bar, and folder names in the scrolling list to locate the file you want to open. (If you don't know how these controls work, see Step 3 in "Edit⇨Create Publisher" earlier in Part III.)

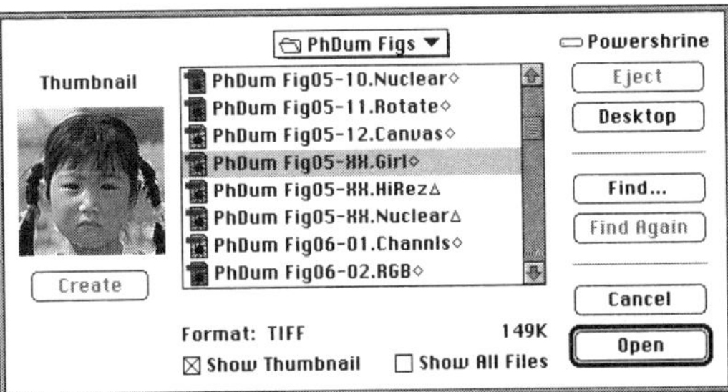

3. If you can't remember where a file is located, but you know its name — or at least part of its name — click on the Find button, enter the part of the name you know, and press Return. Photoshop takes you to the first matching file. To repeat the search, click on the Find Again button.

The keyboard shortcut for the Find button is ⌘-F. The shortcut for Find Again is ⌘-G.

4. Many images include thumbnail previews — which show up on the left side of the scrolling list — so that you can see what the image looks like before opening it. If the image doesn't offer a preview, you may be able to create one by clicking on the Create button under the preview.

If the selected file is saved in any format other than PICT, the Create button is dimmed. (Photoshop lists the file format at the bottom of the dialog box, right above the Show Thumbnail check box.)

The preview won't appear at all if the Show Thumbnail check box is turned off or if QuickTime is not loaded into your system. (QuickTime is a system extension that is installed along with Photoshop.)

5. Normally, Photoshop lists only those files that it knows it can open. Other files are hidden. If you want to see a hidden file and at least try to open it, turn on the Show All Files check box.

When the Show All Files option is selected, a Format pop-up menu appears so that you can specify how Photoshop should open the image.

Unless you know for a fact that a file is saved in a specific format that Photoshop can open, you probably won't be successful. Most folks will want to let Photoshop figure out which files it can open on its own by leaving the Show All Files check box off.

6. Select the file you want to open in the scrolling list.
7. Click on the Open button or press Return. Photoshop opens the image inside a new image window.

Another way to choose the Open command is to press ⌘-O.

File⇨Page Setup

The Page Setup command changes the way the image fits on the page when printing. It has no effect on how the image looks on-screen. To change the on-screen page — called the *canvas* — see "Image⇨Canvas Size" later in Part III.

Choosing File⇨Page Setup displays a Page Setup dialog box that conforms to your specific model of printer. If you're using a PostScript printer, the LaserWriter 8 Page Setup dialog box appears. It offers the widest array of options, so I'll use it as a model.

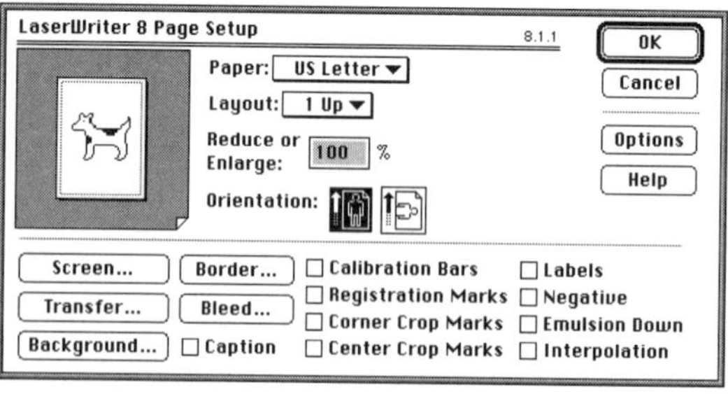

Many options inside any Page Setup dialog box are standardized options inserted by Apple or the printer manufacturer. Therefore, a handful of options have nothing to do with Photoshop, which doesn't always fit the printing mold.

Printer-Specific Option	How You Use It
Paper	Select an option from the Paper pop-up menu to specify the size of the paper on which you want to print the image.

Printer-Specific Option	How You Use It
Layout	PostScript printers let you print multiple pages of a document on a single page. Photoshop doesn't support multiple pages, however, so the Layout option serves no purpose inside Photoshop.
Reduce or Enlarge	Enter a value into this option box to scale the image on the page. Values less than 100 percent reduce the image, which may be necessary if the image is too large to fit on the page.
Orientation	Select one of these icons to print the image vertically or horizontally on the page. If the image is wider than it is tall, for example, select the second icon.
Options and Help	Don't worry about the buttons on the right side of the dialog box, under the Cancel button. They serve a negligible purpose inside Photoshop.

The buttons and check boxes below the gray line are inserted into the Page Setup dialog box by Photoshop. They appear regardless of what model of printer you use.

Many of these options are very advanced and require more explanation than I can deliver in this limited space. However, I can explain the basic function of each so that you understand roughly how they work.

Photoshop-Specific Option	What It Does
Screen	Most printers can print only solid ink or no ink. So in order to represent light shades of colors, such as gray, Photoshop prints tiny dot patterns called *halftones*. You can vary the size and shape of the halftone dots by clicking on the Screen button and modifying the settings in the ensuing dialog box.

(continued)

Photoshop-Specific Option	What It Does
Transfer	Click on the Transfer button to display the Transfer Functions dialog box, which lets you change how various shades in your image print. For example, if an image is printing too dark, you can lighten it by adjusting the curvature of the diagonal line inside the graph so that it dips downward.
Background	To assign a color to the area outside the printed image, click on this button and select a color from the Color Picker dialog box (described in "The Color Controls" in Part I).
Border	To print a border around the current image, click on this button and enter the thickness of the border into the Width option box. The border always appears in black.
Bleed	Imagesetters print to huge rolls of paper or film, so you can print far outside the confines of a standard page size (selected from the Paper pop-up menu). The area outside the page size is called the *bleed*. Click on the Bleed button and specify how far the image can extend outside the page size into the Width option box.
Caption	After entering a caption into the File Info dialog box, you can print the caption along with the image by selecting the Caption check box. For more information about the Caption option, see "File⇨File Info" earlier in Part III.
Calibration Bars	A calibration bar is a 10-step grayscale gradation that starts at 10 percent black and ends at 100 percent black. The function of the calibration bar is to ensure that all shades are distinct and on target.

Photoshop-Specific Option	*What It Does*
Registration Marks	Select this option to print eight crosshairs and two star targets near the four corners of the image. Registration marks are absolutely imperative when you print color separations.
Corner Crop Marks	Select this option to print hairline crop marks in the four corners around the image. These marks tell you how to trim the image in case you decide to engage in a little traditional paste-up.
Center Crop Marks	Select this option to print four pairs of hairlines that mark the center of the image.
Labels	When you select this check box, Photoshop prints the name of the image as well as the name of the printed color channel, which is useful when you're printing color separations.
Negative	When you select this option, Photoshop prints all blacks as white and all whites as black, just like in a photo negative. Imagesetter operators use this option to print color separations to film.
Emulsion Down	The emulsion is the side of a piece of film on which an image is printed. Leave this option to your commercial printer.
Interpolation	If you own an output device equipped with PostScript Level 2, you can instruct Photoshop to soften the printed appearance of a low-resolution image by selecting this option.

File⇨Preferences

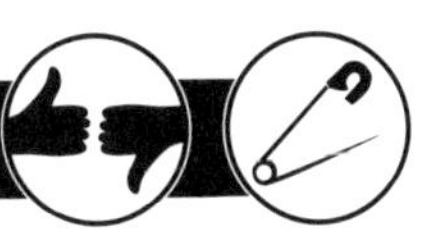

Like all professional-level graphics programs, Photoshop offers a bewildering array of preference settings that you can modify to suit your specific needs and working habits. In Photoshop, you manipulate these settings by choosing commands from the File⇨Preferences submenu.

This submenu offers 10 commands. Luckily, a single one of these — General — contains the preferences you'll be most concerned about. The remaining nine commands are so specialized that you can feel free to ignore them altogether.

When you choose File⇨Preferences⇨General, Photoshop displays the General Preferences dialog box. Click on the More button inside the dialog box to display the More Preferences dialog box, which contains more options that didn't fit in the first dialog box.

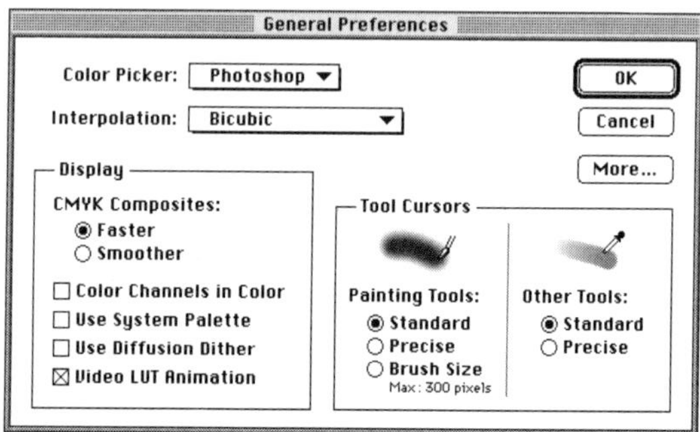

The options from both the General Preferences and More Preferences dialog boxes are explained in the following list:

General Preferences Option	*What It Does*
Color Picker	When you click on the foreground or background color control icon in the toolbox, Photoshop displays one of two color pickers, its own or the one provided by the system software. The former is better, so keep this option set to Photoshop.
Interpolation	When you resize an image using Image⇨Image Size or transform it using one of the commands in the Image⇨Rotate or Image⇨Effects submenu, Photoshop has to make up — or *interpolate* — pixels to fill in the gaps. You can change how Photoshop calculates the new pixels by choosing an option from the Interpolation pop-up menu. However, the best setting is the default setting, Bicubic.

General Preferences Option	What It Does
CMYK Composites	When you edit a CMYK image, you're trying to display CMYK colors on an RGB monitor. You can tell Photoshop to do a better but slower job of translating the colors by selecting the Smoother radio button, or you can speed things up with some small loss in accuracy by selecting Faster. I'd leave this option set to Faster.
Color Channels in Color	Select this option to view an independent color channel in the color it represents. For example, the red channel would appear tinted in red. However, most experts agree that the effect isn't very helpful and does much to obscure your image. So leave this option turned off.
Use System Palette	If you use Photoshop on an 8-bit monitor, you can specify how you want it to dither colors on-screen. By default, Photoshop selects the 256 colors that are most suited to your image. In doing so, however, it must switch color palettes every time you bring a new document to the foreground. If you want all images to use the same color palette, select the Use Diffusion Dither option.
TIP	PowerBook screens are notoriously bad at displaying colors outside the 256 colors in the system palette. So turn the Use System Palette check box on when using a PowerBook; turn it off otherwise.
Use Diffusion Dither	When displaying millions of colors on an 8-bit screen, Photoshop can imitate the colors more accurately if you turn the Use Diffusion Dither option on. You may occasionally see edges between selected and deselected portions of your image after applying a special effect, but it's still a good idea to turn the option on.

(continued)

General Preferences Option	What It Does
	TIP: To eliminate any visual disharmony caused by the Use Diffusion Dither option, you can force Photoshop to redraw the entire image by double-clicking on the zoom tool icon or performing some other zoom function.
Video LUT Animation	This option allows you to preview the effect of various color correction operations on the entire screen without selecting the Preview check box inside the Levels and Curves dialog boxes. Leave this option turned on.
Painting Tools	When you use paint or edit tools in an image, Photoshop can display one of three cursors. Select the Standard radio button to display a cursor that looks just like the tool icon. Select Precise to display crosshairs. But my favorite is the Brush Size option, which shows the actual size of the brush, up to 300 screen pixels in diameter.
	KEY SHORTCUT: When Standard or Brush Size is selected, pressing the Caps Lock key displays the precise crosshair cursors. When Precise is selected, pressing Caps Lock displays the actual brush size.
Other tools	Again, you can select Standard to get the regular cursors or Precise to get crosshairs. I prefer to leave this option set to Standard because you can easily access the crosshairs by pressing Caps Lock.
Image Previews	The More Preferences dialog box starts off with several Image Previews options. The Icon check box creates a tiny preview icon that you can view at the Finder level. The Thumbnail check box creates a larger preview that displays inside the Open dialog box (as explained earlier in "File⇨Open").

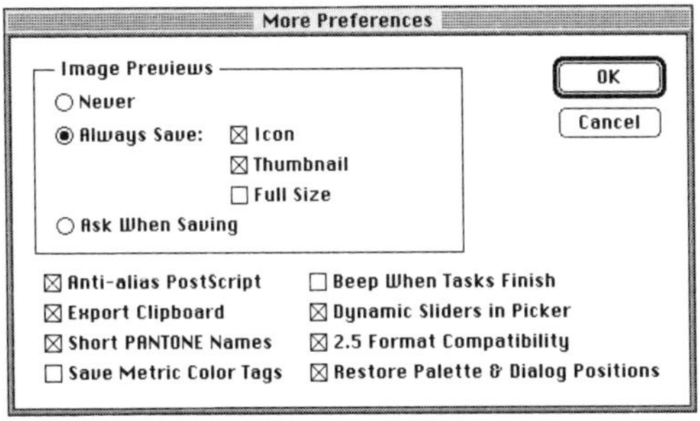

More Preferences

Image Previews
- ○ Never
- ◉ Always Save: ☒ Icon ☒ Thumbnail ☐ Full Size
- ○ Ask When Saving

OK | Cancel

☒ Anti-alias PostScript ☐ Beep When Tasks Finish
☒ Export Clipboard ☒ Dynamic Sliders in Picker
☒ Short PANTONE Names ☒ 2.5 Format Compatibility
☐ Save Metric Color Tags ☒ Restore Palette & Dialog Positions

General Preferences Option	*What It Does*
	The third and newest option, Full Size, creates a 72 dpi preview that can be used for placement inside QuarkXPress.
	If you'd rather decide which previews to assign when saving a file, select the Ask When Saving radio button. All three Image Preview options then appear at the bottom of the Save dialog box.
Anti-alias PostScript	You can copy a path from Illustrator 5.0 or 5.5 and paste it into Photoshop. The Anti-alias PostScript option smoothes out the edges of the pasted paths, so leave it turned on.
Export Clipboard	When selected, this option ensures that Photoshop transfers a copied image from its internal Clipboard to the system's Clipboard when you switch applications. This enables you to paste the image into another running program. Turn this option off if you plan to use copied images only within Photoshop.
Short Pantone Names	Don't worry about this option. It just changes the way Photoshop names Pantone colors when you use a Pantone color in a duotone (discussed later in "Mode⇨Duotone"). Leave it on.

(continued)

General Preferences Option	What It Does
Save Metric Color Tags	If you use EFI's EfiColor for Photoshop to help with screen and printer calibration, and you import and print most of your images inside QuarkXPress, turn this option on. Otherwise, leave it off.
Beep When Tasks Finish	Turn this option on if you want Photoshop to beep at you whenever it finishes an operation that displays a progress window.
Dynamic Sliders in Picker	When selected, this option instructs Photoshop to preview color effects within the slider bars of the Picker palette. Leave it on.
2.5 Format Compatibility	This option saves Photoshop 3.0 files in a way that enables you to open them in Photoshop 2.5. But it also results in larger files. So unless you plan on opening new Photoshop images inside old versions of Photoshop, turn this option off.
Restore Palette & Dialog Box Positions	When this option is selected, Photoshop remembers the location of the toolbox and floating palettes from one session to the next. If you turn this check box off, Photoshop displays the toolbox in the upper left corner of the screen and the Brushes, Layers, and Picker palettes in formation at the bottom of the screen each time you run the program.

You can access the General Preferences dialog box from the keyboard by pressing ⌘-K.

The minor preference commands

The next five commands in the File⇨Preferences submenu aren't particularly difficult to use, but neither are they particularly important. If you go the rest of your life without touching a single one of them, you'll be none the poorer for it. But just for the record, the following list contains brief descriptions about how they work:

Minor Preference Command	*How You Use It*
Gamut Warning	Choose this command to change the color Photoshop uses to represent colors that can't be printed when you choose Mode⇨Gamut Warning (discussed later in Part III).
Plug-Ins	If you moved the external modules from the Plug-Ins folder to some other location, you need to tell Photoshop where you put them using File⇨Preferences⇨Plug-Ins.
Scratch Disks	To allow you to open and edit large images inside limited RAM, Photoshop stores portions of the image in temporary files — called *scratch files* — on disk. If you have multiple hard disks, you can tell Photoshop which disk to use for this purpose using the Scratch Disks command.
Transparency	Any time you view one layer on its own, Photoshop indicates the transparent areas using a checkerboard pattern. You can modify the size of the checks and change their colors using File⇨Preferences⇨Transparency.
Units	Use this command to change the unit of measurement used throughout Photoshop. You can also enter column specifications if you want to match a page created in PageMaker or QuarkXPress. (You would then size the image to the column by choosing the Column option from the Width pop-up menu inside the New or Image Size dialog box.)

The color conversion commands

The last four commands in the File⇨Preferences submenu control how Photoshop translates on-screen RGB colors to printable CMYK colors. The more accurate your settings, the more accurately the printed colors will match their on-screen equivalents.

The only problem is, the commands are so complex that you need the help of a trained printing professional to use them. What follows is only the briefest of introductions to these commands.

Color Conversion Command	*How You Use It*
Monitor Setup	Use the Monitor Setup command to tell Photoshop what kind of monitor you're using so that it knows how you're viewing the RGB colors.
Printing Inks Setup	The Printing Inks Setup command contains options that you use to explain the commercial printing press on which you'll print your full-color image. Your commercial printer is the only one who can help you with this command.
Separation Setup	The Separation Setup command tells Photoshop how to generate black ink from RGB combinations. Again, consult your commercial printer about this one.
Separation Tables	If you use a color management system such as Apple's ColorSync, you can load a custom separation table using this command. This feature eliminates the need for using the Printer Inks Setup and Separation Setup commands.

File⇨Print

Choose File⇨Print to print your image. As with those inside the Page Setup dialog box, the specific options inside the Printer dialog box vary depending on what kind of printer you use. Because a PostScript-compatible printer — such as an Apple LaserWriter — provides the widest variety of options, this is the dialog box I'll use as a model.

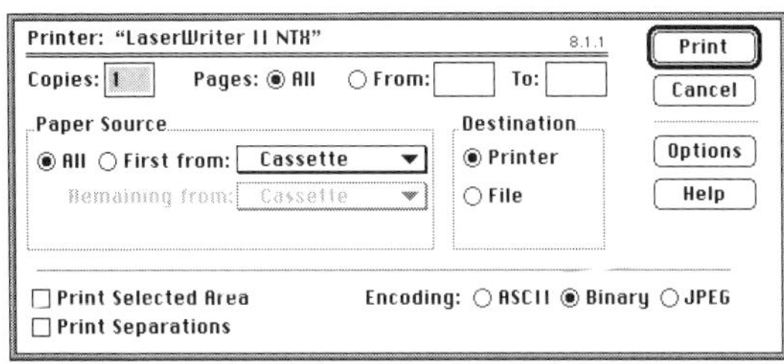

Printing Option	*How You Use It*
Copies	Enter how many copies of the image you want to print into this option box.
Pages	The Pages options are set up for printing long documents from a word processor or page-layout program. An image is never more than one page long, so these options — All, From, and To — have no effect in Photoshop.
Paper Source	If your printer offers multiple paper trays or if you want to manually feed a page through the printer, select an option from the First From pop-up menu. Otherwise, ignore this option.
Destination	The File radio button lets you print an image to a PostScript file on disk. But there's no real point in doing this with an image because Photoshop lets you save to the EPS format, which is a PostScript file. So select the Printer radio button instead.
Print Selected Area	Finally, a useful option! If you have selected a portion of your image, you can print only the selected area by choosing this option.
Print Separations	After converting an image to the CMYK color mode by choosing Mode⇨CMYK Color, you can print color separations, in which each primary color — cyan, magenta, yellow, and black — appears on a separate page. Normally, you'll

(continued)

Printing Option	How You Use It
	want to print separations to film, so leave this option turned off and let your commercial printer worry about it later.
Encoding	This option controls how Photoshop sends data to your printer. Leave it set to Binary.

To print an image, press ⌘-P.

File⇨Place

Choose File⇨Place when you want to import an EPS drawing created in Adobe Illustrator into the image that you're currently working on. Here's how it works:

1. Choose File⇨Place and locate the Illustrator drawing you want to import.
2. Select the file in the scrolling list and click on the Open button or press the Return key.
3. Photoshop displays the imported illustration inside a marquee with four corner handles. Drag the X inside the marquee to move the illustration; drag the handles to scale it.
4. After you scale the illustration and move it into position, move your cursor inside the marquee so that the cursor changes to a gavel. Then click to antialias the image.

After clicking with the gavel, you can still move the imported image because it floats above the image. But you can no longer scale it without harming the image.

File⇨Quit

File⇨Quit closes all open images and quits the Photoshop program. If you've made changes to any image since the last time you saved it to disk, Photoshop asks whether you want to save those changes.

- Press Return to save the changes.
- Click on the Don't Save button or press D to abandon the changes.
- Click on the Cancel button or press Escape to cancel the Quit command and return to the image window.

You can also quit Photoshop by pressing ⌘-Q.

File⇨Revert

The Revert command returns an image to the way it looked when it was last saved to disk. This is the command you choose when everything has gone completely haywire since the moment you opened the image. I use it a lot.

After you choose File⇨Revert, Photoshop asks whether you really want to abandon all the changes you've made since last saving the image. Respond as your conscience directs.

File⇨Save

File⇨Save is the most important command inside any program. It saves the image to disk so that your changes are preserved come rain or come shine. It's your little insurance policy against crashes, system errors, and other computing disasters. Save early and save often.

- If you created the image using File⇨New and you've never saved it before, choosing File⇨Save displays a dialog box that requires you to specify a name, location, and format for the saved file.
- If you opened the image using File⇨Open or you have saved the image before, File⇨Save merely updates the file on disk without bothering you with a dialog box. This is why the Save command has no ellipsis.

The following steps explain how to save an image for the very first time. You can use these same steps to save an image for the second or third time using either File⇨Save As or File⇨Save a Copy.

1. Choose File⇨Save to display the dialog box.

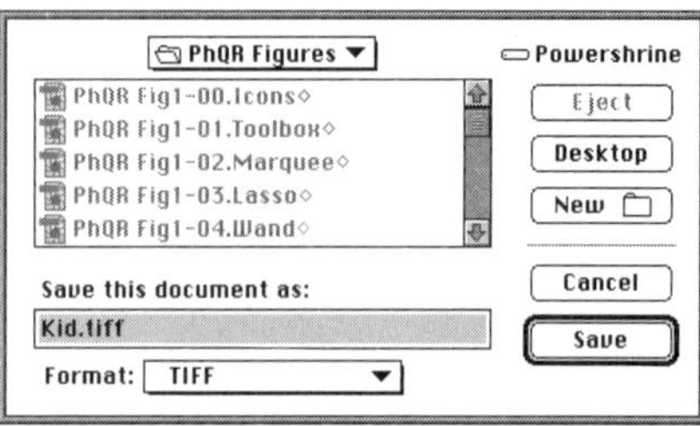

2. Use the Desktop button, folder bar, and folder names in the scrolling list to find the folder in which you want to save the image. (If you don't know how to use these controls, see Step 3 in "Edit⇨Create Publisher" earlier in Part III.)
3. Enter the name of the file into the Save This Document As option box. The name can be up to 31 characters long.
4. Select an option from the Format pop-up menu to specify which file format Photoshop should use to save the image. Photoshop offers access to a ton of formats, but only a few are important:
   - Select the Photoshop 3.0 format if you intend to use the image only in Photoshop or if the image contains layers. (If you want to save an image that contains layers in a format other than Photoshop 3.0, use File⇨Save a Copy.)
   - If you just want to use the image inside Photoshop but you're short on disk space, try the PICT format. This format lets you take advantage of JPEG compression, which modifies the image so that it takes up much less room on disk.
   - If you want to import your image into another program, use TIFF, the best file format on earth.
   - If you want to trade the image with another program but you also want to compress it so that it takes up less room on disk, choose the JPEG format.
   - If you want to import the image into Adobe Illustrator, none of these formats will work. You have to choose EPS instead.
   - Ignore all the other formats. It's highly unlikely that you'll ever need them.

5. Click on the Save button or press Return. Photoshop saves the image to disk as instructed.

The easiest way to initiate the Save command is to press ⌘-S.

Photoshop 3 For Macs For Dummies devotes Chapter 3, "Save Before You Say Goodnight," to the subject of saving. You'll also find more detailed discussions of the top five file formats — Photoshop 3.0, TIFF, JPEG, PICT, and EPS — in that chapter.

File⇨Save a Copy

After you add layers to an image, Photoshop only lets you save it in the Photoshop 3.0 format. Unfortunately, you can't import an image saved in this format into any other program.

The solution to this predicament is File⇨Save a Copy. By choosing this command, you can save a flattened version of the image — with all the image detail but with no distinction between one layer and another — under a different name and using any file format. Just choose the command, enter a name for the file, select a format, and press Return.

The Save a Copy command doesn't change the name of the image in the title bar, nor does it remove the layers from the open image. If you choose File⇨Save, Photoshop continues to save the image in the Photoshop 3.0 format under the old name. The Save a Copy command merely creates a flattened copy of the image on disk.

For the step-by-step rundown of how to save an image using Save a Copy, see the preceding section, "File⇨Save."

File⇨Save As

To save an image under a different name, in a different location, or in a different format, choose File⇨Save As. Photoshop displays the same dialog box it does when you chose File⇨Save for the first time. You use these options exactly as discussed in "File⇨Save" earlier in Part III.

The Save As command is useful for saving a version of an image when you're not sure that you want to get rid of the previous version. It's also great for switching formats in the middle of a job or creating backup copies of an image on a different disk.

Filter⇨Blur

The commands under the Filter⇨Blur submenu make an image blurry. Three of the commands — Blur, Blur More, and Gaussian Blur — simply make an image appear out of focus. The other two — Motion Blur and Radial Blur — make the image look as if it's moving very quickly.

Blur Filter	*How It Works*
Blur	Apply this command to make the image appear slightly out of focus.
Blur More	Blur More makes the image even blurrier.
Gaussian Blur	If you want to control the exact degree of blurriness and experiment with different settings, choose Filter⇨Blur⇨Gaussian Blur, one of Photoshop's most useful filters. The filter displays a dialog box that contains a single option box, Radius. Higher values make the image appear more out of focus. A preview window shows you how the effect will look. When the Preview check box is on, Photoshop also blurs the image in the image window.

Original

Blur

Blur More

Gaussian Blur (1.5 pixels)

Blur Filter	*How It Works*
Motion Blur	The Motion Blur filter makes the image look like it's moving quickly in a linear direction. The Angle value in the Motion Blur dialog box controls the direction of the movement. You can also change the direction by dragging the line inside the circle. Specify how far pixels are blurred in the Distance option box. Higher Distance values produce more dramatic effects.

(continued)

Blur Filter	*How It Works*
Radial Blur	This filter spins an image around in a circle or makes it appear as if it's rushing toward you. You select the kind of movement you want to produce by selecting either the Spin or Zoom radio button, respectively, inside the Radial Blur dialog box. The Amount value determines the distance of the movement. Higher values produce more dramatic effects.  Drag inside the Blur Center box to change the point about which Photoshop spins or zooms the image.

Original

Motion Blur (45°, 10 pixels)

Radial Blur (Spin, 10 pixels)

Radial Blur (Zoom, 40 pixels)

Filter⇨Distort

The commands under the Filter⇨Distort submenu really rip an image apart. As the submenu name suggests, these filters distort images by simulating fun-house mirror and water reflections.

Although these filters are a lot of fun to use, they damage the detail in an image pretty severely. If you plan on applying two or more filters in a row, play it safe by saving your image to disk before choosing a Filter⇨Distort command.

Distort Filter	*How It Works*
Displace	After you choose this filter, Photoshop asks you to locate a grayscale file on disk. The filter then scoots pixels in the selected image based on the shades in the grayscale file. Displace can render some pretty interesting effects, but it requires such a high degree of planning that only a handful of skilled professionals ever use it.
Pinch	Here's a filter for new and experienced users alike. By entering a positive value into the Amount option box inside the Pinch dialog box, you squeeze the image inward. When applied to a face, for example, the Pinch filter shrinks the features and accentuates the forehead and jaw.

(continued)

Pinch (50%)

Ripple (Medium, 100)

Spherize (100%)

Twirl (–100%)

Distort Filter	*How It Works*
Polar Coordinates	This filter produces a dialog box with two radio buttons. The first, Rectangular to Polar, compresses the entire top edge of the image to a single point. Then it fans out the bottom edge to form a circle.
	Polar to Rectangular does just the opposite, effectively ripping an image apart and turning it inside out.
	To get type on a curve, try applying the Rectangular to Polar option to a line of text.

Distort Filter	*How It Works*
Ripple	The Ripple filter makes an image look like it's at the bottom of a pool of rippling water. The Ripple dialog box provides an Amount slider and three Size radio buttons. The Amount value changes the number of ripples; the Size option changes the size of the individual ripples.
Shear	Use this filter to skew an image or make it wiggle back and forth. Click on the grid inside the Shear dialog box to add points to the line. Then drag these points to change the curvature of the line, which directly affects how the image wiggles.
Spherize	The Spherize filter is the opposite of the Pinch filter. Rather than pinching an image inward, it bends it outward, wrapping it onto a sphere. Positive Amount values bend the image outward; negative values bend it inward.
Twirl	This filter twists an image around in a spiral. A positive Angle value rotates the center of the image in a clockwise direction. A negative value rotates the center counterclockwise.
Wave	The Wave filter is basically a supercharged version of the Ripple filter. Unfortunately, it's about 20 times as hard to use as well. The options in the Wave dialog box are so insanely complicated, even Nobel laureates have problems with them. My only advice is to put your faith in the force and experiment blindly. Oh, and select Square from the Type radio buttons if you want to generate random Cubism effects. Look gang, it's Picasso-matic!

(continued)

Distort Filter	*How It Works*
Zigzag	If the image were at the bottom of a shallow pool of water, choosing the Zigzag filter would be the like dropping a pebble in the pool. The filter creates concentric ripple patterns. Inside the Zigzag dialog box, the Amount value changes the size of the ripples and the Ridges value changes the number of ripples. Three radio buttons let you select from different kinds of ripples.

Filter⇨Last Filter

Before you apply any filter to an image, the very first command in the Filter menu is a dimmed command, Last Filter. After you apply a filter, the command changes to the name of the last filter applied.

You can reapply the most recent filter by choosing the first command from the Filter menu or by simply pressing ⌘-F. Photoshop applies the filter using the exact same settings you used the last time.

If the filter normally displays a dialog box of options, you can redisplay this dialog box and modify the settings by pressing ⌘-Option-F. (Or you can Option-choose the first command in the Filter menu.)

Filter⇨Noise

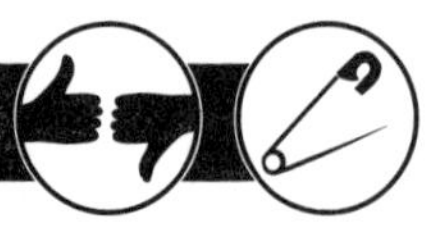

The Noise filters add or delete random pixels — known as "noise" — from an image.

Noise Filter	*How It Works*
Add Noise	If you want to give your image a gritty, earthy quality, you can randomly vary the color of selected pixels using the Add Noise filter.

Noise Filter	How It Works
	The Add Noise dialog box sports an Amount slider. The higher the Amount value, the more noise Photoshop adds to the image.
	The dialog box also offers two Distribution radio buttons. The first, Uniform, creates low-contrast noise. The second, Gaussian, adds more black and white pixels to the image.

Add Noise (32, Uniform)

Add Noise (32, Gaussian)

Noise Filter	How It Works
	To add grayscale noise to a color image, select the Monochromatic check box.
Despeckle	This option eliminates isolated pixels whose colors are inconsistent with surrounding pixels. It's one of Photoshop's least useful filters because it provides no control and rarely performs as you'd like it to.
Dust & Scratches	This filter is supposed to automatically remove dust and scratches from a scanned image. Too bad it doesn't work. More often than not, the filter either blurs the image beyond recognition or smears the dust and scratches so that they look like grease spots.

Noisy Original

Despeckle

Dust & Scratches (1 pixel, 10 levels)

Median (2 pixels)

Noise Filter	*How It Works*
	The better method by far for removing dust and scratches is to use the rubber stamp tool (as explained in Part I) to clone a good portion of your image and use the clone to cover the dust speck or scratch.
Median	The Median filter averages the colors of neighboring pixels. Raise the Radius value in the Median dialog box to thicken the detail in the image.

Filter⇨Other

The Filter⇨Other submenu is a repository for filtering commands that don't belong anywhere else.

Other Filter	*How It Works*
Custom	This is another filter for expert, mathematically adept users only. You enter values into a matrix in order to combine the colors of neighboring pixels.
	You can create four types of effects — blurring, sharpening, edge detection, and color embossing. But you have to have a knack for programming to pull it off.
	If you really want to experiment with the Custom filter, just make sure that the sum of all the values in the center 25 option boxes is always equal to 1.
High Pass	This filter redistributes the light and dark pixels in an image to accentuate the edges. It can be useful for editing masks and creating special effects.
	The High Pass filter contains a single Radius value. This is one of the rare cases where lower values produce more dramatic effects, eventually graying out an image as the filter traces more and more edge detail.
	 After applying the High Pass filter, choose Image⇨Adjust⇨Auto Levels to increase the contrast.

(continued)

High Pass (5 pixels)

Maximum (1 pixel)

Minimum (1 pixel)

Offset (30 pixels right and down, Wrap Around)

Other Filter	*How It Works*
Maximum	The Maximum filter expands white areas in the image. You can use it to expand the selected region in a mask.
Minimum	Maximum's opposite is the Minimum filter, which expands the black areas in an image. Use it to shrink the selected areas in a mask.
Offset	This filter merely scoots an image a specified number of pixels. For example, you might scoot the image 30 pixels to the right and 30 pixels down.

Other Filter	How It Works
	Of course, you can scoot an image by selecting it and nudging it with the arrow keys. The beauty of the Offset filter is that it lets you wrap pixels from one side of an image around to the other side, something that you can't do with the arrow keys. Just select the Wrap Around radio button in the Offset dialog box.
	*Photoshop 3 For Macs For Dummies* features an interesting use of the Offset filter along with Filter⇨Distort⇨Polar Coordinates. See Chapter 20, "Ten Amusing Ways to Mess Up a Loved One's Face."

Filter⇨Pixelate

The Pixelate filters combine pixels in an image to create a special pattern effect.

Pixelate Filter	How It Works
Color Halftone	Choose this command to convert an image into big, comic-book style halftone dots. You specify the size of the dots and the angle of the cyan, magenta, yellow, and black patterns.
Crystallize	The Crystallize filter organizes an image into irregularly sized nuggets, as if you were viewing the image through sculpted glass. You specify the size of the nuggets by entering a value into the Cell Size option box.
Facet	This filter fuses areas of similarly colored pixels to create a sort of hand-painted effect.

Crystallize (10)

Facet

Mezzotint (Medium Lines)

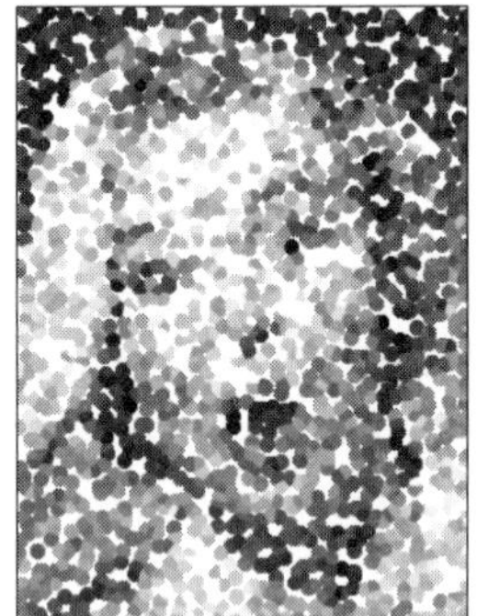

Pointillize (10)

Pixelate Filter	*How It Works*
Fragment	I hesitate to call any Photoshop feature "stupid" because there's always the chance that I just haven't learned how to use it properly. But if there is a stupid filter, it's Fragment. It repeats an image four times in a square formation to create a jiggly effect. Puh-lease.
Mezzotint	A *mezzotint* is a special halftone pattern made up of rough lines and random splotches. When you choose Filter⇨Pixelate⇨Mezzotint, Photoshop permits you to select from ten different patterns. A preview shows how the final effect will look.

(continued)

Pixelate Filter	*How It Works*
	All the Mezzotint options convert the pixels in each color channel to either black or white. This results in a maximum of eight colors in the RGB mode.
Mosaic	An image is already made up of tiny square pixels. The Mosaic filter divides an image into larger squares. All you have to do is enter the size of the squares in pixels.
Pointillize	This filter lays down a pattern of colored circles. The gaps between the circles are filled in with the background color. You specify the size of the circles by entering a value into the Cell Size option box.

Filter⇨Render

The Render submenu contains filters that change the lighting of an image. Two of these filters — Lens Flare and Lighting Effects — can be applied to RGB images only.

To apply Lens Flare or Lighting Effects to a grayscale image, convert the image to the RGB mode (by choosing Mode⇨RGB) before applying the filter. When you're finished, convert the image back to the grayscale mode (Mode⇨Grayscale). There's always a way around the arbitrary barriers.

Render Filter	*How It Works*
Clouds	Apply this filter to fill the entire selection with a random haze of colors ranging from the foreground color to the background color. It doesn't matter what the image looks like before you apply the command; Photoshop replaces it with clouds.

Render Filter	How It Works
Difference Clouds	This command combines the haze created with the Clouds filter with the original image using the Difference blend mode. This inverts the image where the clouds are light and leaves the image unaffected where the clouds are dark.
	TIP Apply the Difference Clouds filter several times in a row — by pressing ⌘-F — to create a marble texture.
Lens Flare	This filter adds sparkles and halos to an image, as if you were pointing the camera directly at a light source when shooting the image. The Lens Flare dialog box provides a Brightness slider — which produces the best results when left at 100 percent — and three radio buttons that create different kinds of flares.
Lighting Effects	Earlier I whined about the complex dialog box that appears when you choose Filter⇨Distort⇨Wave. Well, it's nothing compared with the Lighting Effects dialog box, which shines colored lights on an image as if it were hanging in a gallery.
	The best way to use this filter is to select a predefined option from the Style pop-up menu. You can then experiment with the other options in the dialog box with the assurance that if something goes wrong, you can always return to the original lights by again selecting the Style option.

(continued)

Clouds

Difference Clouds

Lens Flare (100%, 50–300mm Zoom)

Lighting Effects (2 o'clock Spotlight)

Render Filter	*How It Works*
Texture Fill	This filter isn't even a filter. It's merely a companion command to the Light Effects filter. It lets you load an image as a repeating pattern into a channel. Then you can select that channel from the Texture Channel pop-up menu inside the Light Effects dialog box. In other words, ignore Filter⇨Render⇨Texture Fill.

Filter⇨Sharpen

Use the commands in the Filter⇨Sharpen submenu to sharpen the focus of soft or fuzzy scans. I guarantee you, you'll choose the commands from this submenu more frequently than those under any other Filter submenu.

Sharpen Filter	*How It Works*
Sharpen	Apply this command to bring the image into sharper focus.
Sharpen Edges	Choose this filter to sharpen the edges of the details in an image without sharpening the neutral areas. For example, you could sharpen the features in a face without affecting the pores and other skin detail. This sounds great, but unfortunately the filter doesn't handle the task very well. It results in abrupt transitions between sharpened and unaffected areas, which looks unrealistic.
Sharpen More	The Sharpen More command brings an image into crisper focus than the vanilla Sharpen command.
Unsharp Mask	The only way to control the exact degree of sharpening is to choose Filter⇨Sharpen⇨Unsharp Mask. Despite its weird name, this is easily the most practical filter in Photoshop. Enter a value up to 500 percent into the Amount option box to specify the amount of sharpening. Higher values produce sharper images. (Be careful not to oversharpen.) The Radius value determines how many pixels are sharpened at a time. Higher values result in thicker details. Values between 0.5 and 2 are the most common. Higher values result in high-contrast effects.

(continued)

Sharpen

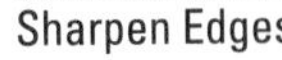

Sharpen Edges

Sharpen More

Unsharp Mask
(200%, 4 pixels)

Sharpen Filter	*How It Works*
	The Threshold value allows you to sharpen some edges without sharpening others. Higher values make the filter more selective. To sharpen the image evenly, leave Threshold set to 0.

If you're interested in learning more about correcting out-of-focus images, read Chapter 16, "Ridding Your Image of Dangerous Toxins," in *Photoshop 3 For Macs For Dummies*.

Filter⇨Stylize

The commands under the Filter⇨Stylize submenu are a fairly ragtag collection. They all produce special effects without distorting the image, combining pixels, or shining lights, which is why they don't appear in the Distort, Pixelate, or Render submenu. However, they're too numerous and too fun to use to be relegated to filter obscurity in the Other submenu. So they're tossed together in the Stylize submenu instead.

Stylize Filter	How It Works
Diffuse	This filter roughs up the edges of an image. You can select the Normal radio button to apply the filter evenly. Or select Darken Only or Lighten Only to apply the effect only when the filtered pixels are darker or lighter than the original pixels.
	Try applying this filter several times in a row to produce progressively rougher results.
Emboss	Emboss makes your image appear as if it were stamped in metal. The edges in the image appear in relief; the other areas turn gray.
	The Angle value determines the direction of the effect. Experiment with this value until you get the effect you want. (There are no right or wrong answers.)
	The Height value defines the size of the embossed edges. Generally speaking, the lower the Height value, the better. I prefer a Height of 1 or 2.
	The Amount value changes the amount of contrast between relief edges and gray non-edges. A higher value results in more contrast.

(continued)

Stylize Filter	How It Works
Extrude	This filter breaks an image into tiles — just like the upcoming Tiles filter — and forces them toward the viewer in three-dimensional space. You specify the size of the tiles and their depth — that is, how far they appear to extend outward.
	TIP: Select the Pyramid radio button to convert the image into a bunch of colored spikes. It's downright kinky.
Find Edges	This wonderful filter traces around the edges of an image with a variable, organic outline. Soft edges become thick outlines; hard edges become thin outlines. Low-contrast areas become white, and high-contrast areas become black.
Solarize	This filter inverts every color lighter than medium gray in an image without affecting the darker colors. It's a simple color mapping technique that creates a quasi-psychedelic effect.
	WARNING! The Solarize filter completely eliminates the light areas in an image. To bring them back, choose Image⇨Adjust⇨Auto Levels.
Tiles	The Tiles filter lets you break up an image into square tiles. You can fill the area between tiles with the background color, the foreground color, an inverted (photographic negative) version of the image, or with the original image itself.
Trace Contour	This command traces single-pixel lines along the borders between light and dark pixels in each of the color channels. You specify where the border lies. For example, if you enter 128 — medium gray — Photoshop traces between the colors darker than medium gray and the colors lighter than medium gray.

Diffuse (Normal)

Emboss (45%, 2 pixels, 300%)

Find Edges

Wind (Wind, Left)

Stylize Filter	*How It Works*
Wind	This filter smears pixels either to the left or to the right. You can select from three Method options — Wind, Blast, and Stagger. Wind produces the most subtle effect; Blast is the strongest. The Stagger option smears pixels randomly back and forth.

Filter⇨Video

The Filter⇨Video submenu provides access to just two filters, both of which are designed to edit images for videotape.

Video Filter	*How It Works*
De-Interlace	Images captured from videotape often appear jiggly because the even and odd scan fields in the video don't align properly. To fix this, choose the De-Interlace filter and experiment with the first two radio buttons. (Leave the second set of radio buttons set to Interpolation.)
NTSC Colors	If you are preparing an image that will be transferred to videotape, you should know that some colors — especially bright reds and blues — may become unstable. To stabilize the colors, choose Filter⇨Video⇨NTSC Colors.

Image⇨Adjust

When you open an image in Photoshop, the colors may not look just the way you had hoped. The image may be too dark, it may appear washed out, or it may have a color cast that makes it look like you're viewing it through colored glasses.

You can correct the colors in the image using the commands under the Image⇨Adjust submenu. Many of these commands do the same thing — they just approach the problem from different angles. For this reason, I recommend that you stick with the commands that do a good job (such as Levels and Variations) and stay away from the ones that don't (namely Brightness/ Contrast, Color Balance, Replace Colors, and Selective Colors).

Color Correction Command	How You Use It
Levels	If you learn how to use only one command under the Image⇨Adjust submenu, it should be Levels. This command lets you precisely manipulate brightness and contrast by changing the whites, blacks, and medium grays in an image. The Levels dialog box contains three Input Levels values. These correspond to the three slider triangles below the histogram (that black birthmark in the center of the dialog box). Drag the first triangle to the right to darken the image; drag the last triangle to the left to lighten it. Move the middle triangle left or right to darken or lighten the medium grays.

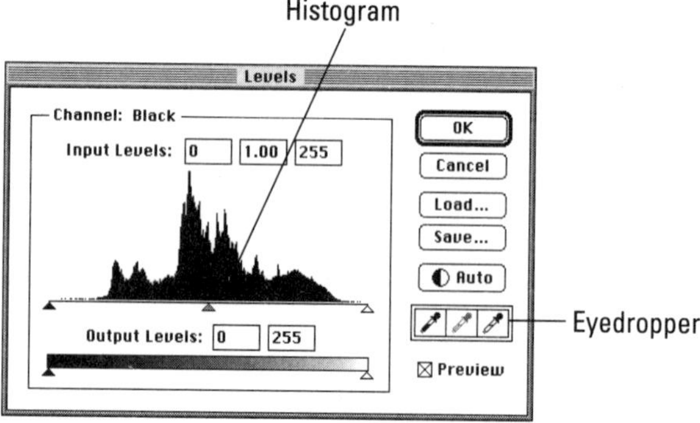

You can also use the eyedropper tools inside the dialog box to change the Input Levels values. Select the first eyedropper and click inside the image window to make the color you click on black. The second and third eyedroppers make the color gray and white, respectively.

(continued)

Color Correction Command	How You Use It
	The Output Levels option boxes correspond to the slider bar at the bottom of the dialog box. Drag the first triangle to the right to lighten the blacks in the image. Drag the second triangle to the left to darken the whites.
	Select the Preview check box to view the effects of your edits in the image window. (When the check box is off, Photoshop applies the changes to the entire screen, assuming that Video LUT Animation in the General Preferences dialog box is turned on.)
	Press ⌘-L to bring up the Levels dialog box.
Curves	Image⇨Adjust⇨Curves is both more powerful and more complex than Levels. Rather than adjusting black, white, and medium gray only, the Curves dialog box lets you change any level of gray in the image.

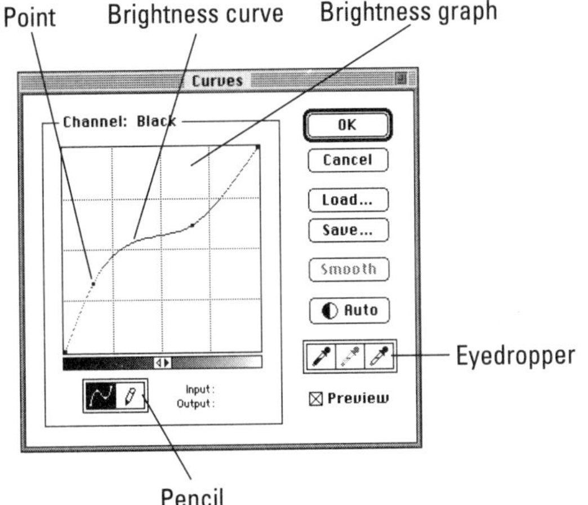

Color Correction Command	How You Use It
	The line through the central brightness graph shows how the colors have been modified. When you start out, the colors have not been modified at all, so the line is perfectly diagonal.
	Click on the line to add a point. Drag the point up to darken the image; drag it down to lighten the image. You can add as many points as you like, so you can lighten some colors in the image and darken others with absolute control.
	Click on the pencil icon to draw a free-form line in the brightness graph. Shift-click to create straight lines between points. If the transitions between colors seems a little harsh, click on the Smooth button to soften the effect.
	You can choose the Curves command quickly from the keyboard by pressing ⌘-M.
Brightness/Contrast	Increase the Brightness value inside the Brightness/Contrast dialog box to increase the brightness of the image. Increase the Contrast value to increase the amount of contrast between lights and darks.
	Although easy to use, this command is not particularly capable. The Levels command offers much more control, if you can come to terms with that command.
	Press ⌘-B to display the Brightness/Contrast dialog box.
Color Balance	The Color Balance command tints portions of a color image using three slider bars, each of which represents a pair of color opposites.

(continued)

Color Correction Command	How You Use It
	Frankly, this command isn't even worth learning. Image⇨Adjust⇨ Variations provides the exact same capabilities in a more straightforward format.
	Even though it's a bad command, you can choose it from the keyboard by pressing ⌘-Y.
Hue/Saturation	This command lets you edit the hue, saturation, and luminosity levels in an image. Change the tint of the image by modifying the Hue value; change how vivid the colors are with Saturation; and lighten or darken the image with the Lightness slider.
	You can also modify specific ranges of colors by selecting the radio buttons along the left side of the dialog box. Select R to edit the reds, select Y for the yellows, and so on.
	To colorize a grayscale image, convert it to an RGB image by choosing Mode⇨RGB Color. Then choose Image⇨Adjust⇨Hue/Saturation, select the Colorize check box, and experiment with the Hue and Saturation sliders.
	You can press ⌘-U to display the Hue/ Saturation dialog box from the keyboard.
Replace Color	This command is a combination of Select⇨Color Range and the Hue/ Saturation dialog box. You're better off learning those two commands and ignoring this one.
Selective Color	If you want to control the amount of cyan, magenta, yellow, and black ink in an image, choose Image⇨Adjust⇨ Selective Color. Photoshop provides this command specifically for prepress professionals. You probably won't find much use for it.

Color Correction Command	How You Use It
Auto Levels	This little command is the miracle cure. If your image looks overly dark, overly pale, or just plain gray, choose Image⇨Adjust⇨Auto Levels. Photoshop automatically changes the lightest colors in the image to white and the darkest colors to black, expanding the color range.

Original

Auto Levels

	Choosing the Auto Levels command performs exactly the same function as clicking on the Auto button inside either the Levels or Curves dialog box.
Desaturate	Use this command to convert a selected area inside a color image to grayscale. For example, if you want to show a black-and-white Dorothy walking through the Technicolor world of Oz, select Dorothy and choose Image⇨Adjust⇨Desaturate.
Variations	Choose Image⇨Adjust⇨Variations to display the enormous Variations dialog box, which is filled with thumbnail previews of the image subject to different color adjustments. Simply click on the thumbnail that represents the color correction you want to make.

(continued)

Color Correction Command	How You Use It
	To make the changes more subtle, drag the slider triangle in the upper right corner of the dialog box toward Fine. To make the changes more dramatic, drag the triangle toward Coarse. Strange, overly bright colors in the thumbnails represent areas that won't print accurately. To view the colors normally, turn off the Show Clipping check box.

For a detailed tour of Photoshop's most essential color correction commands — including Levels and Variations — read Chapter 17, "Drawing Color from a Dreary Wasteland," in *Photoshop 3 For Macs For Dummies*.

Image➪Apply Image

The Apply Image command lets you merge one image with another image. Both images must be open, and they must be exactly the same size, pixel for pixel.

This command is ridiculously hard to use and remarkably inflexible to boot. You'll have far more control mixing images if you do it with layers.

For example, you can use the move tool to drag one image and drop it onto another, as explained in "The Move Tool" in Part I. Then use the options in the Layers palette to mix the two layers together, as described in "The Layers Palette" in Part II.

Image➪Calculations

Image➪Calculations lets you mix specific channels in different images and place the results in a new image window. Calculations is like the Apply Image command in that the channels all have to be exactly the same size. And like Apply Image, Calculations is overly complex and inflexible.

Image editing professionals use the Calculations command to combine masks and other channels. You can also transfer selection outlines from one image to another. But considering that the complexity-to-performance ratio is higher than the Sears Tower, I seriously doubt that you'll want to waste much time on this command.

Image⇨Canvas Size

The Canvas Size command changes the size of the page — or "canvas" — on which the image resides without scaling the image itself.

- If you decrease the size of the canvas, you crop the image, just as if you had used the crop tool (as discussed in Part I).
- If you increase the size of the canvas, Photoshop fills the new, empty area with the background color.

Choose the Canvas Size command to display the Canvas Size dialog box. Enter the new size of the canvas into the Width and Height option boxes. You can change the unit of measure by selecting a new option from the pop-up menu to the right of the option box.

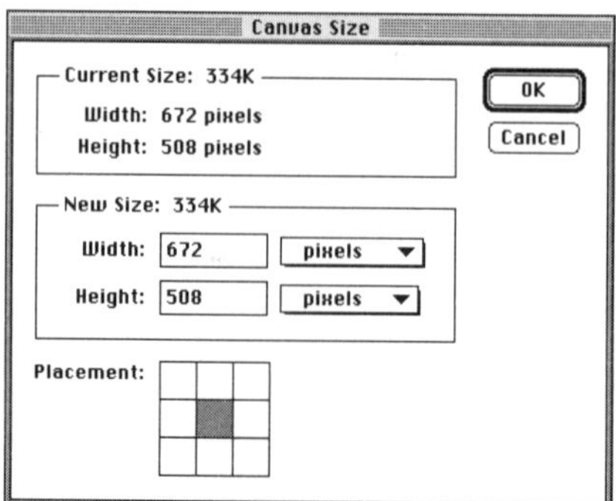

Click inside the Placement grid to specify how the image should sit on the new canvas. For example, if you enlarge the canvas and click inside the upper left square in the grid, Photoshop expands the canvas down and to the right of the image.

To restore the original Width and Height values, Option-click on the Cancel button. (The word Cancel changes to Reset when you press Option.)

You can change the size of the canvas to match the size of any other open image by choosing the image from the Window menu.

Image⇨Duplicate

Choose Image⇨Duplicate to create a copy of the image in a new image window. The duplicate image is completely independent of the original image, allowing you to edit the image in an entirely different direction.

When you choose Image⇨Duplicate, a dialog box asks you to name the new image window. If the image contains multiple layers, you can select the Merged Layers Only check box to merge all visible layers and create a single-layer image.

Press Option when choosing the Duplicate command to bypass the Duplicate dialog box and have Photoshop name the image automatically. Of course, you can always change the name when you save the image to disk.

Image⇨Effects

The commands under the Image⇨Effects submenu allow you to stretch a selected area of the image. Though the commands produce different effects, you use them in the same way:

1. Select a portion of your image and then choose a command from the Image⇨Effects submenu. Photoshop surrounds the selection with a rectangular marquee that has four corner handles.
2. Drag a handle to stretch the image. After you release, Photoshop uses big chunky pixels to approximate the new appearance of the transformed image.
3. Keep dragging the corner handles until you achieve the effect you want.

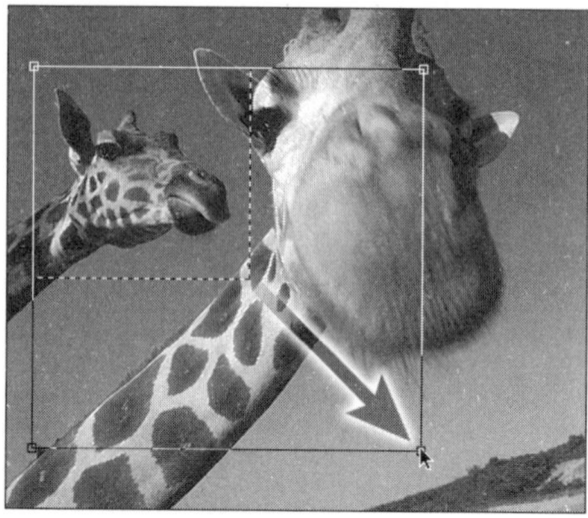

4. Move the cursor inside the marquee. When the cursor changes to a gavel, click to instruct Photoshop to redraw the stretched image.

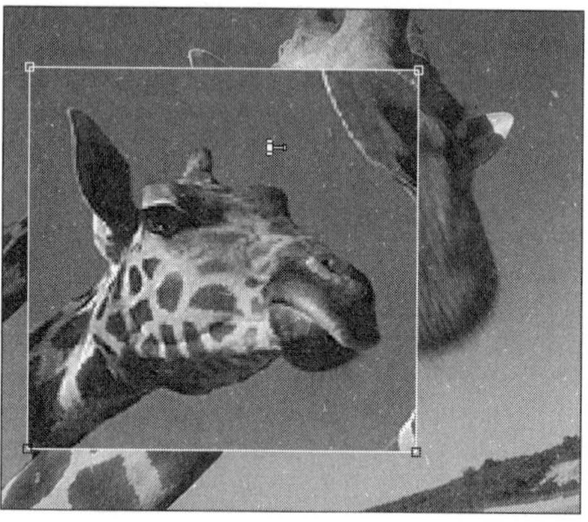

Alternatively, you can click outside the marquee to cancel the transformation.

The following list explains what each of the Image⇨Effects commands does.

Effects Command	What It Does
Scale	Choose this command to enlarge or reduce the selection. Shift-drag a corner handle to scale the selection proportionally — by the same percentage horizontally and vertically. When visible, the Info palette lists the percentage by which the selection has been scaled.
Skew	This command lets you slant an image. Dragging on a corner handle leans the selection in that direction. At first, Photoshop moves two handles together to ensure an orthogonal slant. But after the first drag, you can move the handles independently to simulate a perspective effect. To move two handles together again, Shift-drag a handle.
Perspective	When you choose this command, Photoshop constrains two opposite handles so that they move opposite of one another. The result is a symmetrical perspective effect. To create a perspective effect that is not symmetrical, choose Image⇨Effects⇨Skew.
Distort	The Distort command allows you to move all handles entirely independently of each other. You can stretch the image in absolutely any way you see fit.

Float the selection by choosing Select⇨Float (or pressing ⌘-J) before applying the Image⇨Effects commands. Otherwise, you may leave some background-colored gaps behind the stretched selection.

The Image⇨Effects submenu is dimmed if no part of the image is selected.

Image⇨Flip

The commands under the Image⇨Flip submenu flip the selection or — if no portion of the image is selected — the entire image. Because you can always flip the image back by choosing the command again, these commands are as safe as milk.

Flip Command	*What It Does*
Horizontal	This command flips the image horizontally.
Vertical	This one flips the image vertically, so up is down and down is up.

This is about as simple as Photoshop gets.

Image⇨Histogram

Image⇨Histogram doesn't change your image one iota. Rather, it displays a statistical readout of the image's vital signs, including the total number of pixels and the medium brightness value.

The command gets its name from the graph inside the Histogram dialog box, which shows the distribution of the colors in the image. Each vertical line in the graph represents a brightness value, from black on the left to white on the right. The height of the line represents the number of pixels colored with that brightness value.

To find out information about a specific line in the histogram, position your cursor over it. Three values on the right side of the dialog box tell you the brightness value represented by the line, the number of pixels colored with that brightness value, and the percentage of the image that is darker than this brightness value.

You can examine specific channels by choosing options from the Channel pop-up menu or by pressing ⌘-key shortcuts (⌘-1 for the red channel, ⌘-2 for the green, and so on).

Unless you're a natural gear-head, you probably won't find much use for this scientific image data. But it can be useful for judging the overall lightness or darkness of an image. (To change the distribution of colors, see "Image⇨Adjust" earlier in Part III.)

Image⇨Image Size

The Image Size command lets you change the size or resolution of an image. Image Size is one of the most essential commands in Photoshop, but it's also quite dangerous. You can easily throw away pixels using this command. And as anyone who uses Photoshop on a regular basis can tell you, pixels are the heart, lungs, and circulatory system of an image.

1. Choose the Image Size command to display the Image Size dialog box.

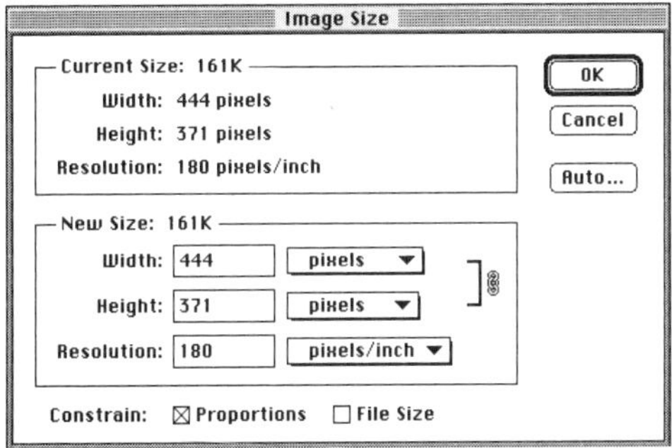

2. To scale the image proportionally — so that the width and height are affected equally — leave the Proportions check box turned on. If you want to change the width or height independently, deselect the check box.
3. Select the File Size check box to ensure that the number of pixels in the image does not change when you adjust the Width and Height values.
4. Enter the new size of the image into the Width and Height option boxes.
5. Change the unit of measure for the Width or Height value by choosing an option from the pop-up menus to the right of the option box.

If the unit is set to either Pixels or Percent, changing the respective Width or Height value changes the number of pixels in the image, regardless of whether the File Size check box is on or off. A higher value adds pixels; a lower value deletes them.

6. Change the Resolution value to alter the number of pixels that print per inch. If the File Size check box is on, changing the Resolution value affects the Width and Height values as well.

Changing the Resolution value has no effect on the on-screen appearance of the image. It merely changes the size at which the image prints. (You can also change the size by adjusting the Reduce or Enlarge value in the Page Setup dialog box, as explained earlier in "File⇨Page Setup.")

7. Click on OK or press Return to change the size and resolution of the image.

To restore the original Width, Height, and Resolution values, Option-click on the Cancel button. (It changes to a Reset button when Option is pressed.) Also worth noting: You can snag the Width, Height, and Resolution values from an open image by choosing the image's name from the Window menu.

For all you ever wanted to know about using Image⇨Image Size — including the mysterious workings of resolution and file size — read Chapter 5, "Pick a Peck of Pixels," in *Photoshop 3 For Macs For Dummies*.

Image⇨Map

Like the commands in the Image⇨Adjust submenu, those in the Image⇨Map submenu change the colors in an image. However, instead of correcting colors, the Map commands produce special effects.

Color Effects Command	*How You Use It*
Invert	This command creates a photographic negative of the image. White becomes black, black becomes white, and all the intermediate colors likewise change to their opposites.  To invert an image, just press ⌘-I.

Color Effects Command	*How You Use It*
Equalize	Like Image⇨Adjust⇨Auto Levels, the Equalize command changes the lightest colors in the image to white and the darkest colors to black. But Equalize also redistributes the other colors in an effort to flatten out the histogram (which you may recall from "Image⇨Histogram" a few pages back).

Original

Invert

Equalize

Posterize (4 levels)

If part of the image is selected, Image⇨Map⇨Equalize displays two radio buttons. If you choose the first — Selected Area Only — the command affects the selection only. If you choose the second — Entire Image Based on Area — Photoshop equalizes the entire image according to the colors inside the selection.

(continued)

Color Effects Command	How You Use It
	You can access the Equalize command by pressing ⌘-E.
Threshold	Threshold changes all selected pixels to either white or black. You enter a value into the Threshold Levels option box or drag the slider triangle under the histogram. All selected pixels darker than the value turn black; all lighter pixels turn white.
	Press ⌘-T to choose the Threshold command.
Posterize	This command reduces the number of colors in an image. You specify the number of colors by entering a value into the Levels option box.
	This command works on a channel-by-channel basis. So if you enter a Levels value of 4 in an RGB image, Photoshop strips each channel down to four brightness values. Four to the third value (for each of the three channels) gives you 64 total colors.

Image⇨Rotate

Choose a command from the Image⇨Rotate submenu to rotate a selection or the entire image. Rotations are measured in degrees. There are 360 degrees in a circle, so 180 degrees equal a half turn and 90 degrees make a quarter turn.

Rotate Command	What It Does
180°	This command turns an image upside-down. (You can get the same effect by choosing Image⇨Flip⇨Horizontal followed by Image⇨Flip⇨Vertical.)
90° CW	Choose this command to rotate the image a quarter turn clockwise (to the right). When no part of the image is selected, this command rotates both image and canvas.

Rotate Command	What It Does
90° CCW	This command does just the opposite of 90° CW, rotating the image a quarter turn counterclockwise (to the left). Again, when the image is deselected, 90° CCW rotates both image and canvas.
Arbitrary	Choose the Arbitrary command to display a dialog box. Enter the number of degrees into the Angle option box and then select whether you want to rotate the image clockwise or counter-clockwise. If the image is deselected, Image⇨Rotate⇨Arbitrary enlarges the canvas to accommodate the rotated image.
Free	This command surrounds the selection with a marquee. Drag a corner handle to rotate the image. You can monitor the degree of rotation in the Info palette. When you finish, click inside the marquee with the gavel cursor. The Free command is dimmed if no portion of the image is selected.

Image⇨Trap

The Trap command spreads colors in a CMYK image to eliminate gaps that may appear if the commercial printing press becomes slightly misregistered. Sunday comics frequently suffer from misregistration when the cyan, magenta, yellow, and black colors don't line up properly.

Luckily, slight registration problems almost never result in gaps in photographic images. And the Trap command can't account for large registration problems.

So why does the Trap command exist at all? It's specifically made for folks who create high-contrast artwork in Adobe Illustrator and then open these images in Photoshop. You choose Image⇨Trap and enter the amount of color overlap you want to create in pixels. Photoshop spreads the colors automatically.

If you don't plan on opening any Illustrator artwork in Photoshop, you're not alone. Few folks do. Furthermore, you have no use for the Trap command.

The command is dimmed except when you're working with a CMYK image.

Mode⇨Bitmap

The Bitmap command converts a grayscale image into an image composed exclusively of black and white pixels. If you plan on printing your image to a laser printer, you can use the bitmap command to create better looking output.

1. If the image isn't grayscale already, choose Mode⇨Grayscale to convert it.
2. Choose Mode⇨Bitmap to display the Bitmap dialog box.

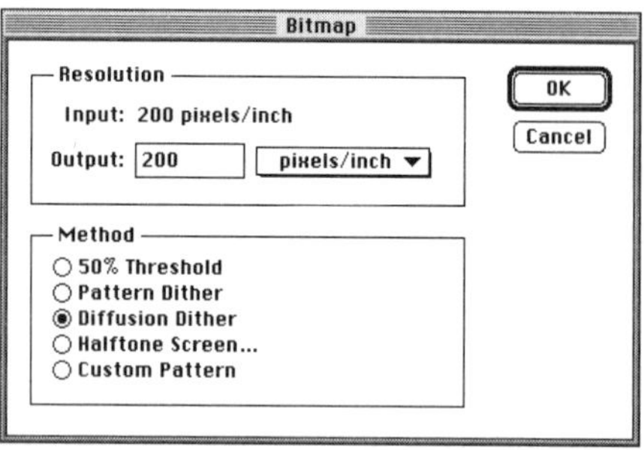

3. The Resolution area lists the present resolution of the image. Raise or lower the Output value to increase or decrease the number of black and white pixels in the image.

If you plan on selecting the Diffusion Dither radio button in Step 4 — generally the best setting for low-end printing — enter an Output value equal to about half the resolution of your printer. If your laser printer prints 300 dots per inch, for example, enter 150 into the Output option box.

4. Select one of the Method radio buttons to specify the halftone pattern Photoshop uses to represent the shades of gray in the image.

   - 50% Threshold makes all colors either black or white, just like Image⇨Map⇨Threshold (discussed earlier in Part III). Unless you have some specific effect in mind, don't select this option.
   - The Pattern Dither option employs a series of predefined dot patterns to emulate fewer than 100 shades of gray. Never in a billion years should you select this option.
   - Diffusion Dither creates a random series of dots to intelligently emulate every one of the 256 gray values. It's a winner every time.

Grayscale

Bitmap (Diffusion Dither)

   - Select the Halftone Screen option if you want to create a pattern of predefined halftone dots and lines. After you click on the OK button, Photoshop presents you with another dialog box of options — the same options it offers when you click on the Screen button in the Page Setup dialog box. Frankly, these latter options are more useful because they convert the image on the fly as it prints rather than permanently altering the image pixels.

- The Custom Pattern option uses a pattern you define by choosing Edit⇨Pattern as a custom halftone dot. Provided that the image is big enough, this option can be fun for creating special effects. If no pattern has been defined, the Custom Pattern radio button is dimmed.

5. Click on OK or press Return to convert all pixels to black or white.

After you convert an image to black and white, you can no longer apply the vast majority of Photoshop's tools and commands. Therefore, be certain that you are done editing your image before choosing Mode⇨Bitmap. And save the black-and-white image under a different name so that you can later return to the grayscale image if you need to make modifications.

Mode⇨Color Table

After choosing Mode⇨Indexed Color to strip an image down to 256 colors or fewer (as explained later in Part III), you can edit the specific colors in the image by choosing the Color Table command.

1. Choose Mode⇨Color Table to display the Color Table dialog box.
2. Click on the color you want to change. Photoshop displays the Color Picker dialog box (explained back in "The Color Controls" in Part I).
3. Edit the color as desired and press Return to go back to the Color Table dialog box.
4. Repeat Steps 2 and 3 for each color you want to edit.
5. When you finish editing, click on OK or press Return.

The problem with this dialog box is that there's no way to know whether the color you select in the Color Table is the color you want to change in the image. Suppose that one flesh tone in the image looks positively green. When you enter the Color Table dialog box, you're presented with 10 or more colors that could be your green flesh. Short of trial and error, you have no way to tell which is the right one.

Mode⇨CMYK Color

Before you print color separations of an image, you have to convert it to the CMYK mode by choosing Mode⇨CMYK Color. Even if you don't plan on printing your own separations, you'll probably want to convert to the CMYK mode so that you can see your colors more or less as they'll actually print.

1. Finish editing your image. The CMYK mode is decidedly slower than the RGB mode, so get as much work out of the way as possible.
2. Choose Mode⇨CMYK Color. Photoshop converts the red, green, and blue channels to four new color channels — one each for cyan, magenta, yellow, and black.
3. Adjust the colors in the image using Image⇨Adjust⇨Levels (as explained earlier in Part III). The CMYK conversion process has a habit of dulling and darkening colors slightly. You can lighten them up using the Levels command.
4. If the image looks a little soft, sharpen it up using one of the commands under the Filter⇨Sharpen submenu.

After you convert to the CMYK mode, do not convert back to RGB. Every color conversion reduces the number and clarity of colors in your image.

Mode⇨CMYK Preview

This wonderful command enables you to preview the effect of converting to the CMYK mode without actually changing any colors in your image. By working in this preview mode, you can accurately gauge how tools and commands will affect the printable colors in your image.

When the CMYK Preview command is on, it has a check next to it. To view the RGB colors again, simply rechoose Mode⇨CMYK Preview.

Mode➪Duotone

A duotone is a special variety of grayscale image printed using multiple inks. Accepted wisdom holds that a single ink can represent anywhere from 50 to 100 unique shades. Meanwhile, a grayscale image contains 256 shades. By combining two inks, you square the number of printable shades, resulting in enough shades to represent a grayscale image.

1. Make sure that you're working on a grayscale image. Choose Mode➪Grayscale if necessary.
2. Choose Mode➪Duotone. The Duotone Options dialog box rises up from the ether.

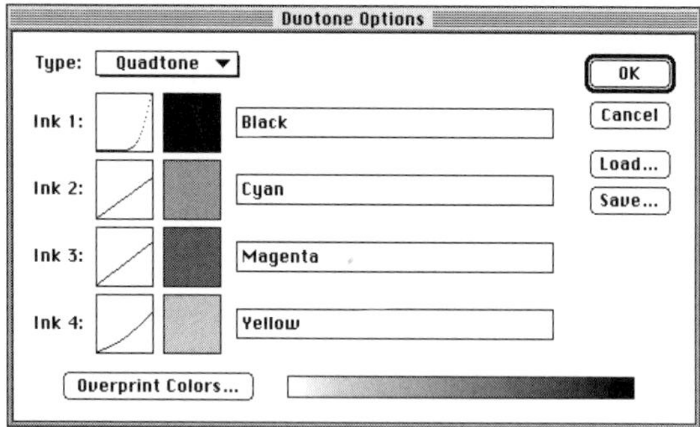

3. Instead of messing about with the options inside this dialog box, it's far easier to open one of the predefined duotones that ship with Photoshop. Click on the Load button and locate the Duotone Presets folder inside the Goodies folder (in the same folder that contains the Photoshop program).

   You'll see three more folders — Duotone, Tritone, and Quadtone. Select the folder that corresponds to the number of inks you want to use — two, three, or four, respectively. Two is more than sufficient. Then enter the Process Duotones folder, select one of the files, and press Return. The 30 or so available files all offer different settings; experiment to see which is best.

4. Click on OK inside the Duotone Options dialog box or press Return to apply the inks to the image. Photoshop applies a slight tint to the image — it's extremely subtle on-screen. But it will make a heck of a difference when you print the image.

If you want to import the duotone into PageMaker or QuarkXPress, you need to save it in the EPS format (as explained in "File⇨Save" earlier in Part III).

Mode⇨Gamut Warning

Choose this command to make all the colors that cannot be printed appear gray on-screen. (Colors that cannot be printed are said to be "outside the CMYK gamut," hence the command name.) The actual pixels are not affected; they merely appear gray as long as the command is turned on.

You can then select the out-of-gamut colors and modify them or drag over them with the sponge tool to lower their saturation.

To turn the command off and return the pixels to their normal appearance, choose Mode⇨Gamut Warning again.

You can choose the Gamut Warning command inside the Color Picker dialog box to gray out nonprinting colors inside the color field. (As you may recall from Part I, you display the Color Field by clicking on either the foreground or background color icon in the toolbox.) This way, you can easily eliminate certain colors and concentrate just on the printing ones.

Mode⇨Grayscale

Choose this command to convert a color image to the grayscale mode.

- If you choose Mode⇨Grayscale while viewing all colors in an RGB, Lab, or CMYK image, Photoshop blends the channels to create a grayscale version of the image.
- If you go to a single color channel by clicking on an item in the Channels palette (as explained in Part II), Photoshop throws away the hidden channels and retains only the visible channel, which is itself a grayscale image.

Therefore, you may want to examine the individual color channels — by pressing ⌘-1, ⌘-2, and so forth — to see if any of them would make a nice grayscale image. When you locate one you like, choose Mode⇨Grayscale.

Photoshop displays a message to make sure that you want to dispose of the colors in the image. Press Return to complete the grayscale conversion and kiss the colors good-bye.

Mode⇨Indexed Color

The Indexed Color command reduces the number of colors in your image to 256 or fewer. You might use this command when preparing an image that will be included in an on-screen presentation.

1. Choose Mode⇨Indexed Color to display the Indexed Color dialog box.

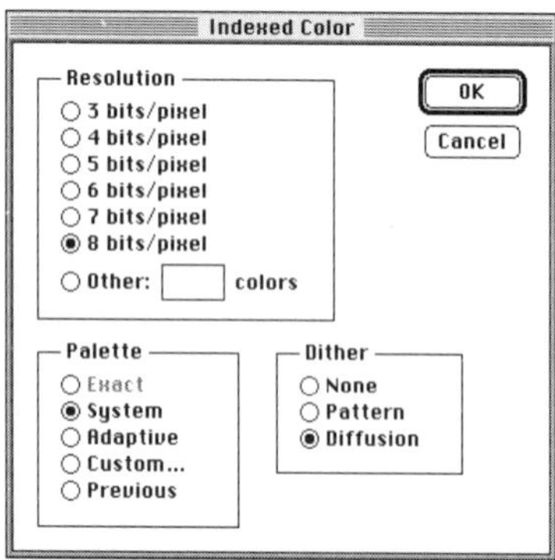

2. Select the number of colors you want to retain from the Resolution radio buttons. Select 8 Bits/Pixel to retain 256 colors, 7 Bits/Pixel for 128 colors, 6 Bits/Pixel for 64 colors, and so on, down to 3 Bits/Pixel for 8 colors.

   Alternatively, you can enter the specific number of colors you want to retain in the Other option box. If the image already contains 256 or fewer colors, Photoshop automatically enters an Other value.

3. Select the colors you want Photoshop to use.
   - The Exact option is dimmed unless the image already contains fewer than 256 colors. Select this option to retain the present colors of the pixels in the image.
   - Select the System option to use the Apple system palette. This palette is the safest because it's used by the Finder and other system-level programs.
   - If you select Adaptive, Photoshop automatically chooses what it considers the best colors to represent your image.
   - Select Custom to display the Color Table dialog box, which allows you to specify every color you want to use. What a lot of work!
   - The Previous option lets you use whatever color palette you used the last time you chose the Indexed Color command.
4. Select the manner in which you want Photoshop to try to emulate other colors in the image. The None option simply converts each color to its nearest indexed color. Pattern uses a geometric pattern. And the best option, Diffusion, applies a random pattern that looks very natural.
5. Click on OK or press Return to convert the image.

As with a black-and-white image created by choosing Mode⇨Bitmap, an indexed image is off limits to many of Photoshop's tools and commands, most notably those under the Filter menu. So be very sure that you're done editing the image before you choose Mode⇨Indexed Color.

You can modify the colors in an indexed image by choosing Mode⇨Color Table, as described earlier in Part III.

Mode⇨Lab Color

The Lab color mode is theoretically capable of representing every color the eye can see. Though the mode is harder to work in than either RGB or CMYK, it allows you to edit virtually without fear of color degradation. And you can easily convert back and forth between the RGB and Lab modes without harming the image.

To convert an image to the Lab mode, choose Mode⇨Lab Color.

Mode⇨Multichannel

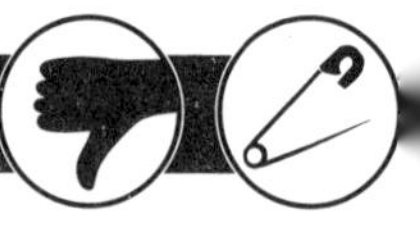

Choose Mode⇨Multichannel to split up all the color channels in an image so that they are no longer related. All channels are treated by Photoshop as mask channels.

Why split up channels? Well, you might reorder them in the Channels palette and then recombine the channels by choosing RGB Color or one of the other Mode commands. But in truth, the chances of you ever finding a practical use for Mode⇨Multichannel are about a billion to one. Feel free to ignore it.

Mode⇨RGB Color

This command converts an image to the RGB mode, the color mode in which you'll do most of your editing. The most common use for this command is to convert a grayscale image before colorizing it. You can also convert a Lab image to the RGB mode.

Select⇨All

Choose this command to select the entire image. You can then copy the image (Edit⇨Copy), cut it (Edit⇨Cut), draw an outline around it (Edit⇨Stroke), float it (Select⇨Float), and do all those other things that you can't do to a deselected image.

To choose Select⇨All from the keyboard, press ⌘-A.

Select⇨Color Range

The Color Range command is like a magic wand tool on steroids. It allows you to select areas of an image according to color. But it's unlike the magic wand in that you can adjust the sensitivity of the Color Range command and preview the results immediately, making it a much more predictable and satisfactory selection tool.

The Color Range command also selects all occurrences of a color in an image, not just continuous areas of the color.

1. Choose Select⇨Color Range to display the Color Range dialog box.

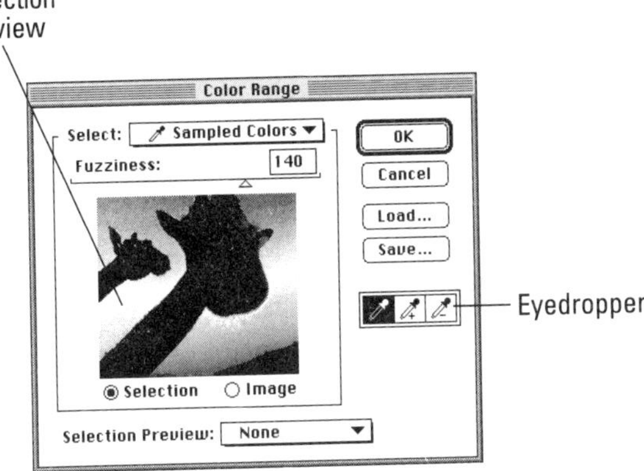

2. Set the Select pop-up menu to Sampled Colors, the default and by far most useful setting. This option lets you specify the colors you want to select.

   (The other Select pop-up menu options limit you to predefined color ranges that you can just as easily specify for yourself.)

3. Click inside the image window to specify the color that you want to select. Your cursor automatically changes to an eyedropper.

   The selection preview in the middle of the dialog box shows the selection as a mask. White pixels in the mask represent portions of the image that will be selected. Black pixels represent deselected areas.

4. If you want to select additional colors, Shift-click on them in the image window. (You can also click with the eyedropper tool that has the plus sign — on the right side of the dialog box — but Shift-clicking is so much easier.)

5. To deselect colors, ⌘-click in the image window. (Again, you can do the same thing by clicking with a different eyedropper tool — the one with the minus sign — but why bother?)

6. Increase the Fuzziness value to increase the size of the selection and soften the selection boundaries. Decrease the Fuzziness value to create more hard-edged selections.
7. Continue to experiment with Shift-clicking, ⌘-clicking, and changing the Fuzziness value. If at any time you want to reset the selection, just click inside the image window to select a single color.

   You can also Option-click on the Cancel button (which changes to a Reset button when the Option key is down).
8. When you are satisfied with the selection, click on the OK button or press Return.

Select⇨Feather

To soften the boundaries of a selection outline, choose Select⇨Feather. A dialog box with a single option box, Feather Radius, appears. You can enter any value up to 250, measured in pixels. The higher the value, the fuzzier the selection outline.

The only problem with the Feather command is that it provides no preview. So you have to guess what Feather Radius value is going to work best (generally, it's somewhere between 6 and 12). If you don't like the result, you can make the selection fuzzier by choosing Select⇨Feather again, but you can't make it less fuzzy.

The Feather command is dimmed if the image is not selected.

Select⇨Float

Select⇨Float is one of the most incredible commands inside Photoshop. All it does is clone the selection and float it above the surface of the image. But after a selection is floating, it is temporarily independent of the rest of the image.

- You can apply multiple filters to the floating selection. If you don't like the outcome, just press the Delete key. Because the selection was floating, the original image remains intact and unharmed by your edits.

- After manipulating the floating selection, you can blend it with the original, underlying image either by changing the Opacity setting in the Layers palette or by choosing a blend mode from the palette's pop-up menu.
- If you want to make the floater permanently independent of the rest of the image, you can convert it to its own layer. Just Option-double-click on the *Floating Selection* item in the Layers palette (as discussed in "The Layers Palette" in Part II).

Watch out for operations that defloat the selection. Deselecting the image defloats it, of course. You also defloat a selection if you clone it by Option-dragging, modify the selection outline by Shift-dragging, or enter the quick mask mode. Most surprising, choosing Edit⇨Stroke defloats a selection. In any case, after you defloat a selection, it becomes adhered to the image, making your changes permanent.

When a selection is floating, the Float command in the Selection menu becomes Defloat. Choose this command to set the image down.

You can access both the Float and Defloat commands from the keyboard by pressing ⌘-J.

Press the Option key when choosing Float (or press ⌘-Option-J) to float a selection without cloning it, leaving a background-colored hole in its wake. When a selection is floating, Option-choosing Defloat (or pressing ⌘-Option-J) sets a copy of the selection down and at the same time keeps it floating.

Select⇨Grow

This command incorporates more colors into a selection. It is most useful in combination with the magic wand tool, allowing you to expand the magic wand selection into areas the wand missed on the first go-around. In fact, the Grow command judges colors based on the Tolerance value in the Magic Wand Options palette (discussed in Part I).

1. With the magic wand tool, click inside the area you want to select. Photoshop automatically selects the image based on the color you clicked on.

2. Did the magic wand miss some areas you wanted to select? Press Return to highlight the Tolerance value in the Magic Wand Options palette.
   - If you want to add just a few more colors to the selection, lower the Tolerance value.
   - If the selection is much too small, raise the value.
3. Choose Select⇨Grow to incorporate more colors into the selection based on the colors inside the selection and the Tolerance values.

Obviously, this command has the same limitations as the magic wand tool. You can't preview the results, so if the selection is too large, you have to undo it and try again. In fact, it's not much more helpful than simply changing the Tolerance value and reclicking with the magic wand.

Despite its mediocre performance, Select⇨Grow is blessed with a keyboard shortcut, ⌘-G.

Select⇨Hide Edges

I probably use this command 100 times a day. It lets you hide the marching ants around a selection so that you can better gauge how the selection and surrounding image match up.

Though the marching ants disappear, the selection remains selected. To bring the marching ants back, choose Select⇨Show Edges.

Press ⌘-H to choose either the Hide Edges or Show Hides command.

Select⇨Inverse

This wonderfully simple command reverses the selection: Everything that was selected is deselected, and all deselected areas become selected.

You can achieve the exact same effect by inverting the mask in the quick mask mode (by choosing Image⇨Map⇨Invert or pressing ⌘-I).

Select⇨Load Selection

This command allows you to convert a mask channel to a selection outline. You can also load a channel from a different image, as long as the image is open and exactly the same size — pixel for pixel — as the image you're working on.

But there's really no point in using this command. It's much easier to Option-click on a mask channel in the Channels palette or press ⌘-Option plus the number of the channel. Both techniques are discussed in "The Channels Palette" in Part II.

Select⇨Matting

The commands under the Select⇨Matting submenu are designed to mix the edges of a floating selection or layer with the image below it. In theory, the commands remove halos around floating images that may make your image less believable. In practice, they simply don't work, not a one of them.

Just the same, the following are descriptions of each of the commands, just in case you want to waste some time with them.

Matting Command	*How It Works*
Defringe	This command takes the antialiased pixels around the edges of the floating or layered image and replaces them with pixels from the background image. The result is more often than not a bunch of ugly streaks around the edge of the image.
Remove Black Matte	If you copy an image from a black background and paste it against a white background, you can choose this command to make the black halo a little less pronounced.
Remove White Matte	This command diminishes the white halo around an image copied from a white background and pasted against a black background.

If the selected area of the image is not floating, the Matting submenu is dimmed. The command is also dimmed when you're working on the Background layer with the image deselected.

Select⇨Modify

The commands under the Select⇨Modify submenu allow you to automatically adjust the boundaries of a selection outline. All four of these commands defloat a floating selection, and they are exclusively applicable to selections.

Modify Command	*How It Works*
Border	Choose Select⇨Modify⇨Border to select an area around the outskirts of the selection outline. You enter the width of the new selection into the Border dialog box — up to 64 pixels — and Photoshop does the rest.
Smooth	To smooth out the corners in a selection outline — particularly one drawn by Option-clicking with the lasso tool — choose the Smooth command. Enter a value up to 16 pixels into the Smooth dialog box. A value around 2 or 3 is best.
Expand	This command increases the size of the selected area by a specified number of pixels.
Contract	Expand's opposite, this command decreases the size of the selection by a specified number of pixels.

If no portion of the image is selected, the Select⇨Modify submenu is dimmed.

Select⇨None

Choose Select⇨None to deselect all selected portions of an image. This command also defloats floating selections.

You can undo Select⇨None by choosing Edit⇨Undo None or pressing ⌘-Z.

You can also press ⌘-D to access this command. You can also deselect an image by clicking in the image window with either the marquee or lasso tool.

Select⇨Save Selection

Choose this command to save the selection to a mask channel. You can even save the selection to a new image or to some other open image that is exactly the same size as the image you're working on.

Most of the time, however, it's much easier to simply click on the convert selection icon in the bottom left corner of the Channels palette (as explained in "The Channels Palette" in Part II).

This command is dimmed if the image is not selected.

Select⇨Similar

Select⇨Similar selects all colors in the image that are similar to the currently selected colors. The command judges similarity according to the Tolerance value in the Magic Wand Options palette (discussed in Part I). The higher the Tolerance value, the more colors Photoshop selects.

To select only those colors that are identical to the colors inside the existing selection, set the Tolerance value to 0 and choose Select⇨Similar. For example, if you selected a portion of a blue sky with the magic wand tool but the rest of the sky is cut off by a big cloud, choosing Similar with the Tolerance set to 0 would select only those blues on the other side of the cloud that exactly match the currently selected blues.

Window⇨Open Images

Photoshop lists all the open images at the bottom of the Window menu. Choose one of these commands to bring the image window to the foreground so that you can work on it.

You can also simply click inside a background image window to bring it to the foreground. (This technique works when you're using any tool other than the eyedropper.)

Window⇨New Window

Choose Window⇨New Window to create a new view of your image. This command does not create an independent copy of the image. That's the job of Image⇨Duplicate (explained earlier in Part III). Rather, it allows you to view a single image from two different perspectives.

For example, with two windows showing the same image, you can magnify one window so that you can see a detail at the 1:1 zoom ratio and zoom out the other window to take in the entire image all at once. You can get an up-close and bird's-eye view of an image at the same time.

You can also view separate channels and hide and display different layers. Any Photoshop function that affects view can be applied to the windows independently. Any function that changes the colors of pixels in the image is reflected in both windows.

Window⇨Palettes

The commands in the Window⇨Palettes submenu enable you to hide and display palettes on-screen. If a command says *Show,* it displays the palette. If it says *Hide,* it closes the palette.

Each Window⇨Palettes command is discussed along with the palette it hides or displays in Part II.

Window⇨Show Rulers

Choose Window⇨Show Rulers to display a horizontal ruler along the top of the image window and a vertical ruler along the left side of the window.

You can change the unit of measurement displayed in the rulers by choosing the Palette Options command from the Info palette menu or by choosing File⇨Preferences⇨Units. Better still, click and hold on the mouse coordinates icon in the Info palette — the third icon down — and select a new measurement from the pop-up menu.

You can change the ruler origin — the point at which all measurements are zero — by dragging from the upper left corner of the rulers into the image window. Release at the point where you want to position the origin.

Press ⌘-R to hide or show the rulers.

Window⇨Zoom Factor

Choose this command to magnify the image to a specified zoom ratio. Inside the Zoom Factor dialog box, select either the Magnification or Reduction radio button to magnify or reduce the image, respectively. Then enter a value between 1 and 16 into the Factor option box and press Return. Photoshop zooms the image as instructed.

Window⇨Zoom In

Choose this command to magnify the image to the next higher zoom ratio. For example, if the zoom ratio is 3:1, choosing Window⇨Zoom In magnifies it to 4:1.

As long as the Never Resize Windows check box in the Zoom Options palette is turned off, as it is by default, the Zoom In command both magnifies the image and expands the image window to fit. This is in contrast to the zoom tool, which magnifies the image but has no effect on the window.

To choose Window⇨Zoom In from the keyboard, press ⌘-plus. Option-choose Window⇨Zoom In or press ⌘-Option-plus to magnify the image to the maximum zoom ratio, 16:1.

Window⇨Zoom Out

The Zoom Out command reduces the view size to the next lower zoom ratio. Like the Zoom In command, Zoom Out both reduces the image and resizes the image window to fit.

Press ⌘-minus to choose the Zoom Out command from the keyboard. Press ⌘-Option-minus to zoom out all the way, to the 1:16 zoom ratio.

Index

• Symbols •

• A •

• B •

• C •

• D •

• E •

• G •

• H •

• I •

• J •

• K •

• L •

• M •

• N •

• O •

• Q •

• R •

• S •

• T •

• U •

• V •

• W •

• Z •

IDG BOOKS WORLDWIDE REGISTRATION CARD

RETURN THIS REGISTRATION CARD FOR FREE CATALOG

Title of this book: Photoshop 3 For Macs For Dummies Quick Reference

My overall rating of this book: ❑ Very good [1] ❑ Good [2] ❑ Satisfactory [3] ❑ Fair [4] ❑ Poor [5]

How I first heard about this book:

❑ Found in bookstore; name: [6] ❑ Book review: [7]
❑ Advertisement: [8] ❑ Catalog: [9]
❑ Word of mouth; heard about book from friend, co-worker, etc.: [10] ❑ Other: [11]

What I liked most about this book:

What I would change, add, delete, etc., in future editions of this book:

Other comments:

Number of computer books I purchase in a year: ❑ 1 [12] ❑ 2-5 [13] ❑ 6-10 [14] ❑ More than 10 [15]

I would characterize my computer skills as: ❑ Beginner [16] ❑ Intermediate [17] ❑ Advanced [18] ❑ Professional [19]

I use ❑ DOS [20] ❑ Windows [21] ❑ OS/2 [22] ❑ Unix [23] ❑ Macintosh [24] ❑ Other: [25] ______ (please specify)

I would be interested in new books on the following subjects:
(please check all that apply, and use the spaces provided to identify specific software)

❑ Word processing: [26] ❑ Spreadsheets: [27]
❑ Data bases: [28] ❑ Desktop publishing: [29]
❑ File Utilities: [30] ❑ Money management: [31]
❑ Networking: [32] ❑ Programming languages: [33]
❑ Other: [34]

I use a PC at (please check all that apply): ❑ home [35] ❑ work [36] ❑ school [37] ❑ other: [38] ______

The disks I prefer to use are ❑ 5.25 [39] ❑ 3.5 [40] ❑ other: [41] ______

I have a CD ROM: ❑ yes [42] ❑ no [43]

I plan to buy or upgrade computer hardware this year: ❑ yes [44] ❑ no [45]

I plan to buy or upgrade computer software this year: ❑ yes [46] ❑ no [47]

Name: Business title: [48]
Type of Business: [49]
Address (❑ home [50] ❑ work [51]/Company name:)
Street/Suite#
City [52]/State [53]/Zipcode [54]: Country [55]

❑ **I liked this book!**
You may quote me by name in future IDG Books Worldwide promotional materials.

My daytime phone number is ______

IDG BOOKS®
THE WORLD OF COMPUTER KNOWLEDGE

Please keep me informed about IDG's World of Computer Knowledge. Send me the latest IDG Books catalog.

NO POSTAGE
NECESSARY
IF MAILED
IN THE
UNITED STATES

BUSINESS REPLY MAIL

FIRST CLASS MAIL PERMIT NO. 2605 FOSTER CITY, CALIFORNIA

IDG Books Worldwide
919 E Hillsdale Blvd, STE 400
Foster City, CA 94404-9691